The Enneagram as Living Process

The Architecture of Transformation

John Harper

First Edition: December 2025

ISBN: 979-8-9924438-8-2 (Paperback)

HarpGnosis Books

Dedication

To the spelunkers of the psyche,
the mechanics who keep lifting the hood,
the puzzle-masters who know every piece fits somewhere,
and the sleuths who follow the faintest trace of truth

To all who investigate the inner world with curiosity, courage, and
unreasonable devotion—
this book is for you.

Table of Contents

Introduction

You've felt it before—that moment when a familiar reaction rises in you like clockwork—the tightening in your chest. The words you didn't choose but that chose you. The way your attention narrows or scatters, following grooves worn smooth by repetition. You recognize the pattern even as you're living it, yet the recognition changes nothing. The groove plays on.

This is not failure. This is the machinery of personality—intelligent, ancient, and nearly invisible. We mistake these patterns for ourselves because they run so deep. But they are not who we are. They are what happens when awareness fails to enter at a critical moment, when the natural flow of life encounters interruption and finds another way forward.

The question is not whether you have a pattern. Everyone does. The question is whether you are the pattern or the awareness that can see it.

This difference—between being the pattern and witnessing it—is the difference between a lifetime of sophisticated self-improvement and actual liberation. One keeps you redecorating the prison cell. The other shows you the door was never locked.

So rather than a map of who we are, the Enneagram shows how we got here. It reveals the precise moments when consciousness contracted, the specific thresholds at which flow became fixation, and—most importantly—the exact pathways through which awareness can return. When understood as process rather than personality, the symbol stops being a description of our limitations and becomes a guide to their dissolution.

You could study personality types for decades and remain imprisoned by your pattern. You could memorize all nine types, understand the dynamics, recognize yourself and others with impressive accuracy—and none of it would set you free. Knowledge about the pattern is not the same as seeing through it. Analysis of the cage doesn't open the door.

But when you understand the Enneagram as living process—when you see the actual mechanism by which consciousness forgets and remembers itself—something else becomes possible. You begin to recognize the pattern not as who you are but as a structure you've been inhabiting. You start to catch the moment of contraction as it happens, before it solidifies into identity. The space between stimulus and reaction, which was once imperceptible, becomes inhabitable.

This is not self-improvement. This is recognition of what you always were beneath the pattern.

This exploration returns to the Enneagram's origins as a symbol of universal process, as taught by G.I. Gurdjieff and further developed by J.G. Bennett. Later in the book, we'll explore the nine types through this original lens—not as identities.

We're not dismissing the nine types. We're revealing what they actually are: nine specific ways in which the universal process of descent and return is interrupted in early development. Nine ways the soul adapted when presence was not yet recognizable through self-reflection. Nine variations of the same event—the shock of separation and the longing for reunion.

This approach differs from personality-focused systems not in content but in emphasis. We're looking at the symbol's architecture first, with type as an application rather than a foundation. We're interested in the geometry of how consciousness works—how it descends into form, identifies with that form, and finds its way back to presence. The types are important not because they define us but because they show us where we're still asleep.

When you understand this distinction, three things become possible that self-knowledge alone cannot provide:

1. **Compassion replaces judgment.** When you see that your pattern formed as an intelligent response to a loss of awareness—that it was consciousness adapting creatively to survive separation—you stop treating it as a personal failure. The One's criticism protected rightness when rightness felt threatened. The Four's longing preserved depth when simple belonging was lost. The Eight's control maintained strength when vulnerability seemed dangerous. Each pattern is evidence of the soul's fierce determination to keep what matters most from being lost altogether. Recognizing this dissolves shame at its root.

2. **The work becomes precise.** When you understand where the flow was interrupted—at which specific threshold your pattern crystallized—you know exactly where to bring attention. You're not trying to fix everything or transcend your humanity. You're meeting the precise point where

consciousness can re-enter. This makes transformation practical rather than mystical, immediate rather than distant. The shock points that once produced automatic reaction become the doorways through which presence returns.

3. **Effort becomes unnecessary.** When you stop trying to transcend the pattern and simply see it, the energy that built the personality becomes available for its dissolution. You discover that awareness itself does the work. The same force that created the contraction releases it. This is not passive resignation or spiritual bypassing—it's the recognition that transformation happens through seeing, not through doing. The pattern loosens its hold not because you defeat it but because you illuminate it.

The symbol contains both the architecture of forgetting and the pathway through which we remember. It shows that personality is not a mistake to be corrected but a frozen moment within a larger process—a process that was never actually broken, only interrupted. When awareness returns to the places where it once failed to enter, the flow resumes naturally. What was repetition becomes renewal. What was cage becomes current.

This exploration brings that larger picture into focus. We'll examine the symbol's geometry—the circle, hexad, and triangle, and what each reveals about how energy actually moves through time. We'll identify the two critical thresholds at which consciousness either contracts into personality or opens into presence, and how to recognize these shock points as they arise in daily life. We'll trace how each of the nine types formed around specific losses and specific adaptations, and how those same patterns contain the seeds of their dissolution.

We'll see how the arrows connecting the points describe not movement from type to type but resonance within a single field—how your pattern pulls in defensive qualities when awareness is lost and essential qualities when presence returns. We'll understand why certain relationships trigger your reactivity so consistently and how two people working consciously can transform friction into mutual awakening.

Most importantly, we'll map the stages of the journey from unconscious identification through recognition to living from essence—not as theory but as lived experience you can verify. We'll provide not techniques or practices but invitations to direct recognition, ways of meeting the pattern that allow it to reveal itself and release its grip.

This is not another personality system. This is not about becoming a better version of your type. This is about discovering what remains when the type becomes transparent—the awareness that was always here, witnessing the whole dance, never actually trapped by the pattern it was temporarily identifying with.

The Enneagram is a mirror. Not of who you are, but of how consciousness moves—how it forgets itself through identification and remembers itself through presence. When you understand it this way, the symbol stops being a map of nine different people and becomes a single map of how Being rediscovers itself in time.

The door was never locked. The pattern was never you. What you're seeking has been here all along, witnessing your search.

This exploration invites you to see that for yourself.

The Enneagram as a Process-Symbol

Long before the Enneagram was used to describe personality, it functioned as a technical symbol of transformation. In Gurdjieff's teaching, it encoded the fundamental laws by which anything real comes into being, develops, changes course, and completes itself. Modern typology is a later adaptation—a useful one, but far removed from the symbol's original purpose.

What the Symbol Was Designed to Reveal

For Gurdjieff, the Enneagram was not a diagram of traits but a living map of process. It illustrated how forces arise, interact, lose momentum, and require renewal. He taught that no process—whether building a cathedral, cooking a meal, or cultivating a soul—unfolds without the principles expressed in the symbol. Its value was practical: it showed how things actually work.

The Two Laws at the Heart of the Symbol

Gurdjieff said the Enneagram expresses two universal laws:

1. **The Law of Three.** Every phenomenon arises from three forces: the initiating, the resisting, and the reconciling. Western thinking usually works with dualities, but creation requires a third force—expressed in the Enneagram's inner triangle.
2. **The Law of Seven.** Nothing progresses in a straight line. Every process develops in an uneven rhythm, like a musical octave with its two intrinsic gaps. These "intervals" are where momentum fades unless a new quality enters. This explains why intentions collapse, habits reassert themselves, and transformation demands conscious shocks. This pattern is expressed in the six-pointed movement of the hexad.

A Single Operative Machine

When the triangle (three forces) and the hexad (sevenfold rhythm) interlock within the circle (wholeness), the Enneagram becomes a working symbol rather than a static diagram. It does not describe personality; it reveals the mechanics of becoming. Its function is not explanation but transformation.

A Tool to Be Used, Not Observed

Gurdjieff treated the Enneagram as an instrument. It was meant to be applied to thinking, action, and inner work. It showed where effort is needed, where attention must enter, where a process naturally falters, and where a finer quality of presence must appear. He referred to it as a *legominism*—not information, but technology designed to preserve essential knowledge across generations.

Why Understanding Requires Being

Gurdjieff insisted the Enneagram cannot be grasped through thought alone. Its meaning becomes visible only through the development of attention, sensation, emotional clarity, and presence. The symbol does not describe reality conceptually; it reveals how reality moves. To understand it is to perceive the three forces within one's experience and to observe the sevenfold rhythm operating in one's functioning.

A Map of Transformation, Not Identification

In its original use, the nine points did not refer to personality types. They marked nine positions in the movement of a process—locations where energy shifts, meets resistance, or requires conscious intervention. The points describe the unfolding of a dynamic, not categories of identity. In this sense, the Enneagram is a blueprint for awakening, not a taxonomy of traits.

How This Differs from Modern Typology

The personality Enneagram is a later overlay—valuable, but partial. It identifies where the flow of consciousness contracted in early development and how those contractions solidified into a habitual style. But the original symbol was concerned not with classification but with the movement of energy, the entry points for presence, and the architecture of change.

The Enneagram began as a cosmic formula, a process map, a symbol of transformation, and a living machine. It expresses how anything real is created, how it unfolds, and how it completes itself. It is not a symbol of who you are. It is a symbol of how reality works.

And now that the symbol has been returned to its original function—as a map of movement rather than a catalogue of types—we can step into its first gesture. Every process the Enneagram describes begins where all processes begin: with the circle, the whole field of Being through which everything unfolds.

The Circle

The outer circle of the Enneagram represents the full spectrum of consciousness through which life moves. It is continuous and complete, symbolizing both origin and destination. Moving around the rim, we trace the natural arc of existence: an impulse arises, unfolds, expresses, reflects, questions, renews, embodies, and returns to unity before beginning again.

This is not metaphor. Every experience—from a single breath to the span of a lifetime—follows this pattern. Each point along the rim corresponds to a particular quality of Being, a specific way consciousness shows itself in form. The circle pulses with creation.

- **Point One** – The first spark of intention. Intelligence organizing itself into coherence. The seed of manifestation, the impulse for rightness and order.

- **Point Two** – Love flowing outward. The current extends toward connection, feeling the joy of relationship. Creation begins to embrace otherness.

- **Point Three** – Action flowering. Energy takes shape as movement and expression. Doing becomes the language through which essence enters the world.

- **Point Four** – Self-awareness awakening. The current turns inward, sensing its depth. The soul begins to know itself as sensitivity and individuality.

- **Point Five** – Understanding crystallizing. Awareness functions through perception and thought. Being explores itself through curiosity and clarity.

- **Point Six** – The search for ground. Consciousness seeks trust within not-knowing. Questioning gives rise to faith and the capacity for commitment.

- **Point Seven** – Imagination renewing. Awareness expands beyond the known, moving toward possibilities. The cycle prepares to rise.

- **Point Eight** – Power embodying. Energy grounds itself in strength and presence. Spirit becomes flesh; awareness takes form as autonomy in expression.

- **Point Nine** – Stillness returning. All movement resolves into unity. Awareness rests in itself, whole and silent, ready to begin again.

This sequence describes not steps to follow but the unfolding of life itself. Every moment contains the full circle in miniature—beginning, expression, reflection, return.

Yet something more is happening here. The circle is not only cosmic; it's fractal. Every person studying the Enneagram exists somewhere along this arc, but that "somewhere" is never isolated. It contains the entire pattern in miniature, like a Mandelbrot set repeating itself infinitely within itself. The same geometry governs every scale.

A single breath carries this pattern. A single choice. A single conversation. Each unfolds through the same rhythm: impulse, expression, pause, return. The personality type we identify with is simply one habitual loop within the larger design—a place where awareness fell asleep and the process began repeating mechanically.

Being "a type" means being caught in a smaller orbit within the greater circle. The current of transformation still moves through us, but we've lost sight of the overarching arc. We live as fragments of the total rhythm, spinning in self-similar loops, unaware of the whole that contains them.

The work of self-understanding begins when we remember that the small circle of personality lives within the larger circle of Being. We see that the same intelligence that created the pattern can also free it. Awareness reconnects the fragment to the whole, and what once felt like running in circles begins to feel like turning toward home.

The outer circle reveals the natural arc of becoming, yet this arc is not uniform. Two subtle thresholds interrupt its momentum—places where the current must be met consciously rather than carried by its own force. The first threshold appears as the movement shifts from outward expansion to inner sensitivity, the moment between Points 3 and 4 when doing begins to turn back toward being. The second arises between Points 6 and 7, where the mind's capacity to analyze has reached its limit, and a finer quality must enter for renewal to occur.

At these intervals, the flow cannot continue on its own. Something more delicate than willpower is required. When awareness enters, the movement deepens, and the cycle unfolds into its next octave. When it does not, the current bends inward, and the system repeats its familiar orbit. These two thresholds are the shock points—the places where presence enters or the pattern closes in on itself.

You're driving, not thinking about anything in particular, and suddenly the sky catches your attention—the exact color of blue at this hour, the quality of light on the buildings. For a moment, you're just seeing, no commentary, no you interpreting the scene. Just this. That's Point Nine becoming briefly transparent—awareness resting in itself before the current moves again.

Why the Circle Requires the Triangle

The circle shows the whole field of being through which all experience arises. But wholeness alone cannot account for movement. The moment the circle breathes—the moment being expresses itself in time—three fundamental orientations appear: emergence, recession, and the field that holds them both. These three forces, represented by the inner triangle, are what allow the undivided whole to become dynamic without breaking its unity.

The triangle doesn't sit beside the circle as a separate structure. It arises from it—the first differentiation within totality, the minimal architecture required for movement to have direction, depth, and ground.

The Triangle

At the center of the Enneagram sits the inner triangle, connecting Points 9, 3, and 6. This triangle represents the three fundamental forces that create and sustain everything that exists: awareness, action, and receptivity. Every process—from a breath to a thought to the evolution of a soul—arises from the interplay of these three.

- **Point 9** corresponds to awareness, the reconciling presence that holds all opposites in unity. It is the still center, the timeless background against which all movement occurs.
- **Point 3** represents the active force, the energy of doing and creating. It is the impulse that brings possibility into manifestation.
- **Point 6** represents the receptive force, the openness that allows the new to enter. It is trust, faith, and the willingness to receive what cannot be produced by effort alone.

The triangle is the eternal dynamic force of manifestation. These three forces exist in constant interplay, driving the entire system. The active force of 3 flows into the receptive field of 6. From that openness, reconciliation arises at 9, where awareness holds both activity and surrender in a single field. From 9, presence infuses the next act of creation, as a coherence of continuity.

Why These Three Points Are Different

The triangle types (3, 6, 9) function differently from the hexad types (1, 2, 4, 5, 7, 8). The hexad types represent the stages of descent and ascent—the journey of consciousness through manifestation. The triangle types represent the *forces that enable* that journey.

Think of it this way: The hexad is the river; the triangle is what makes the river flow.

Every point on the hexad requires all three forces to operate. Point One needs awareness (9), action (3), and receptivity (6) to express its quality of rightness. Point Four needs all three to access authentic depth. Without the triangle, the hexad would be a static description rather than a living process.

This is why the three triangle types often report feeling less "fixed" than other types, or why they can seem harder to type. They're not primarily stages in the process of manifestation—they're the underlying forces that animate all stages. The Three doesn't just *do*; it *is* the principle of doing. The Six doesn't just receive; it *is* the opening itself. The Nine doesn't just rest; it *is* the awareness that holds everything.

The Triangle Types in Reactivity

When these three forces fall out of balance, personality forms around their distortion:

- When **Type Three** loses contact with awareness (9) and receptivity (6). Action becomes compulsive doing. The Three performs without presence, achieving without receiving, creating without rest. Success replaces Being.

- When **Type Six** loses contact with awareness (9) and action (3). Receptivity becomes anxiety. The Six questions without ground, seeks safety without trust, opens to threat rather than grace. Faith collapses into vigilance.

- When **Type Nine** loses contact with action (3) and receptivity (6). Awareness becomes passive. The Nine witnesses without participating, holds without engaging, rests without renewing. Peace becomes inertia.

Each triangle type represents one force disconnected from the other two. Personality forms when the three forces that should work together become isolated from each other.

The Triangle Types in Presence

When awareness returns, these same three discover their essential nature:

- **Type Three** reconnects with awareness and receptivity. Doing arises from presence. Action includes rest. Achievement becomes creative expression rather than identity. The Three discovers it can stop and still be real.

- **Type Six** reconnects with awareness and action. Receptivity becomes faith. Questions arise from curiosity rather than fear. The Six discovers trust as immediate knowing and finds it can act from that ground without needing certainty first.

- **Type Nine** reconnects with action and receptivity. Awareness becomes engaged. The Nine discovers it can participate fully while remaining present. Peace includes vitality. Stillness moves.

Point Six as the Portal

Among the three forces, Point Six plays a unique role. At both shock points of the outer circle, the triangle feeds new energy into the process—and Point Six is the gateway through which that force enters.

- Between **3 and 4**, awareness from Point 9 enters through the receptivity of Point 6, reconnecting doing with Being. Without Six's opening, the soul cannot turn inward consciously. It simply contracts.
- Between **6 and 7**, creative force from Point 3 enters through that same receptive channel, renewing the process with inspiration and grace. Without Six's surrender, the mind exhausts itself. Grace cannot enter a closed system.

This is why Six is positioned where it is—why it sits at the second shock point and why it connects directly to both 9 and 3. Six is not just one force among three; it is the hinge between the timeless (9) and the temporal (3). It is the place where "thy will be done" becomes actual lived experience.

The Six's journey from fear to faith is therefore everyone's journey. Every type must learn to receive what cannot be produced, to open when effort has reached its limit, to trust the process rather than control it. The Six lives this threshold more consciously than other types.

The Phobic-Counterphobic Split

Other types display a range of expression—gentle or forceful, inward or outward—but these variations all arise along a single line of contraction. Their strategy never changes direction; it only intensifies or softens within the same pattern. Six alone divides its reactivity into two opposite orientations. Its position at the gateway between the two shock points exposes it to two different incoming forces—awareness from Point Nine and creative will from Point Three. When consciousness is absent, these forces cannot be integrated, and the Six splits into phobic and counterphobic reactions. No other type faces this structural dilemma, which is why Six alone manifests as two fundamentally different styles.

When consciousness is not present to integrate these two currents, Six splits between them.

- **The Phobic Six** forms when Six is oriented primarily toward receiving from Point 9—but reactively rather than consciously:

The phobic Six seeks the reconciling force of awareness through external ground. Unable to rest in its own being, it looks for stability in authority, structure, belief systems, or allegiance to something larger than itself. The receptivity that should open to direct knowing becomes dependency on external certainty.

"If I can just find the right teacher, the right system, the right belief, I'll be safe." The Six merges with what it trusts, tests that trust obsessively, and when trust fails, searches for the next source of ground. This is Point 9's awareness distorted into seeking peace through compliance.

- **The Counterphobic Six** forms when Six is oriented primarily toward receiving from Point 3—but reactively rather than consciously:

The counterphobic Six seeks the active force through assertion and challenge. Unable to rest in uncertainty, it acts—sometimes aggressively—to prove strength, test limits, demonstrate courage. The receptivity that should open to creative grace becomes compulsive doing to manufacture confidence.

"If I can just act strong enough, confront danger, challenge authority, I'll be safe." The Six pushes against what it fears, forces courage through performance, and exhausts itself through constant testing. This is Point 3's creativity distorted into aggression, proving "I'm not afraid."

Both Are the Same Pattern

Phobic and counterphobic are not different types. They are the same Six trying to solve the same problem—lost trust in Being—by drawing on different forces reactively. The phobic Six collapses toward 9's energy without awareness. The counterphobic Six forces 3's creative principle without presence. Both are Six attempting to create safety when the natural ground of faith has been lost.

Many Sixes oscillate between these two poles, sometimes within the same day. In one situation, they'll seek external authority (phobic); in another, they'll challenge authority aggressively (counterphobic). The split is not between two kinds of Sixes but between the two forces trying to flow through Six while consciousness is absent.

The Integration

When Six functions as the conscious portal it's designed to be, something entirely different emerges, the split dissolves.

The Six can receive from Point 9 (awareness) without collapsing into a state of dependency. There's direct knowing, immediate trust, faith that doesn't require external validation. The Six rests in uncertainty without needing to resolve it.

Simultaneously, the Six can receive from Point 3 (creative action) without forcing courage. Action arises naturally from ground rather than from fear. There's real action—not performed but present, not aggressive but clear.

When both forces flow through Six consciously, faith emerges as their integration: a grounded presence that can act. The Six discovers it can question without doubting, engage without forcing, and trust without merging. The receptivity becomes what it was always meant to be—openness to what cannot be produced by effort alone.

This explains why Six alone exhibits the phobic-counterphobic bifurcation. It's not pathology; it's evidence of Six's unique structural position. Six literally has two currents trying to flow through it. When unconscious, Six splits between them, manifesting as two seemingly opposite strategies. When conscious, Six integrates them, becoming the living demonstration that trust and action, stillness and engagement, are not opposites but complementary forces in one field.

The Six's journey from fear to faith is therefore the journey of learning to be the portal consciously—allowing both awareness and action to flow through without identifying with either, without forcing one or collapsing into the other. This is why the Six's transformation matters for all types: it shows what becomes possible when receptivity becomes conscious.

The Triangle as the Living Engine

The inner triangle is the engine of the whole system. It generates the three primordial forces that enable any movement. Awareness at Point Nine recognizes what is happening. Action at Point Three brings impulse into expression. Receptivity at Point Six opens the field, allowing something new to enter. These three forces—the seeing, the doing, and the allowing—form the living engine that animates every process.

If the triangle is the engine, the hexad is the transmission. It is the pattern that takes the raw power of these three forces and channels it into actual movement—directing how the process descends, gathers momentum, weakens, renews itself, and rises again. The hexad determines *how* the unfolding occurs, the specific sequence by which energy shifts direction and becomes experience.

And what we normally call "energy" in the system—the movement that weakens at the two shock points, the momentum that continues or collapses—is the fuel that runs through the hexad. The energy is not the engine itself; it is what the engine generates and what the transmission carries forward.

The three forces of the triangle create the possibility of movement. The hexad gives that movement its pathway. The energy running through the hexad is the fuel that drives the process along that path.

Together, they form a single living mechanism—engine, transmission, and fuel—revealing both how consciousness moves and how it awakens.

This cycle repeats at every scale—in a single breath, in a conversation, in a lifetime. When all three forces work together, the soul's movement becomes fluid. Force circulates freely between rest and activity, between receiving and expressing, between being and doing.

Point Six as the Portal of Renewal

The hexad shows energy moving in one direction: descending into form, condensing into manifestation. But at two critical thresholds—the shock points at 3-4 and 6-7—this descending flow requires new force to continue. Without it, the process simply repeats mechanically. With it, transformation becomes possible.

This is where the triangle feeds the hexad. At both shock points, force enters through Point Six—the receptive portal. Between 3 and 4, awareness from Point 9 flows through Six, reconnecting action with Being. Between 6 and 7, creative impulse from Point 3 flows through Six, renewing the process with inspiration.

What changes is not the direction of flow but the quality of what flows through. When consciousness is present at these portals, essential force (presence) enters the system. The descent becomes ascent without reversing direction—the same pattern now vibrates at a higher frequency. When consciousness is absent, mechanical energy perpetuates the pattern. The flow continues, but nothing transforms.

Six is the gateway precisely because it is receptivity itself—the opening through which what cannot be produced by effort alone can enter. The other eight types follow the hexad's sequential flow. Six stands at the threshold where that flow either closes in on itself or opens to something beyond itself.

The hexad types show us what is unfolding. The triangle types show us how it unfolds. Understanding both gives us the complete picture: the stages of the journey and the forces that move us through them.

The Role of the Inner Figures

The hexad and triangle within the circle, showing how their interaction creates the shock points and the flow of transformation.

Inner Figure	Points	Function in the Process	Energetic Quality
Triangle	9–3–6	The eternal interplay of awareness (9), action (3), and receptivity (6); the living engine of transformation	Balances being, doing, and allowing
Hexad	1–4–2–8–5–7	The hidden rhythm beneath the surface; channels energy through alternating expansion and contraction	Keeps the circle alive through descent and return

Why 3–6–9 Must Be Equidistant

The triangle is not an arbitrary placement of three points on the circle. Its geometry expresses a fundamental truth: the three forces of emergence, recession, and the field must stand in perfect equilibrium for the system to hold together. If even one force were closer to or farther from another, the entire architecture of movement would collapse into duality. Equidistance is essential because it prevents the dominance of any single force.

Emergence, if placed too close to recession, would collapse expression back into absorption before form could appear. Recession, if placed too close to the field, would dissolve experience prematurely into spaciousness. And the field, if positioned unevenly, would either overpower the other forces with stillness or fail to provide the necessary ground for their movements. Only a perfect 120-degree spacing allows the three forces to function as independent yet interdependent movements within the whole.

This equal spacing also provides system stability. Each force has room to articulate itself without immediately triggering its counterpart. Emergence can move outward without being pulled back immediately. Recession can move inward without losing its reference point. The field can hold both movements without collapsing into either. The equidistance of 3–6–9 is what allows the dynamism of the triangle to remain balanced, rhythmic, and recursive.

The geometry of the triangle is therefore not decorative. It expresses the minimal structure required for Being to move without fragmenting. It ensures that illumination, absorption, and ground stand in symmetrical relation, allowing the breath of consciousness to cycle naturally. This is why the triangle remains the gravitational center of the enneagram and why the entire system depends on the precise spacing of these three points.

Core Dynamics Beneath Personality

A Note on Object Relations, Instincts, and Primary Emotions Within the Triangle

The discussion of object relations, instincts, and emotions that follows is not a commentary on the nine Enneagram personality types. It is rooted in the deeper architecture of the inner triangle. The forces expressed at Points Three, Six, and Nine—emergence, recession, and the field—operate long before personality takes shape. They are primordial orientations of Being, and the object relations, instincts, and primary emotions simply reveal how these forces first enter embodiment. We are not describing traits of types but the universal movements that later become patterned through personality.

Every person, regardless of type, engages all three object relations, all three instincts, and all three primary emotions. Idealizing, rejecting, and frustrating are not exclusive to specific types; they are the earliest relational impressions created when the three forces of the triangle encounter the human environment. Likewise, the social, sexual, and self-preservation instincts do not belong to certain types. Still, they are biological articulations of the same forces—each instinct being the body's attempt to carry emergence, recession, or the field into lived expression.

The same triadic pattern is found in the three primary emotions. Shame, fear, and anger are not typological signatures but emotional contractions of the three forces. Shame is the contraction of emergence into self-image. Fear is the contraction of recession into vigilance. Anger is the contraction of the field into bodily reactivity. Each emotion expresses how the organism reacts when one of the primordial forces becomes interrupted or distorted in early experience.

What varies from person to person is not whether these forces operate, but how they manifest—how they contract, adapt, or remain open depending on history, temperament, and the specific interruptions met at the two shock points. Personality is simply the later crystallization of these early relational, biological, and emotional movements. The triangle is the ground; the types are the patterned elaborations. Understanding the object relations, instincts, and emotions at the level of the forces clarifies how all human experience—emotional, relational, somatic, instinctual, and psychological—is shaped triadically from the beginning.

The Enneagram of Personality Types explicates how personality adapts to and expresses these core dynamics, resulting in long-standing patterns of behavior and identification. What we commonly call a "type" is the organism's particular way of managing the three forces, negotiating the three instincts, and living within the three primary emotional fields. Personality does not create these movements—it forms around them. The types reveal the patterned strategies through which these deeper dynamics become organized, fixated, and eventually experienced as "me."

PRIMARY OBJECT RELATIONS

The inner triangle—3, 6, and 9—is often treated as a metaphysical symbol or abstract diagram. Yet these three points also correspond directly to the three primary object relations in developmental psychology: idealizing, rejecting, and frustrating. These are not psychological overlays. They are the earliest disturbances in the relational field, and they map with precise fidelity onto the three fundamental dynamisms of the triangle: emergence, recession, and the field.

These object relations reveal the first interruptions in the breath of Being—the primordial rhythm by which consciousness expresses itself, receives itself, and rests in itself.

Idealizing and Point Three (Emergence)

Emergence is the outward force of Being—the natural radiance moving from depth into expression. In *Good Vibrations: Primordial Sounds of Existence*, this radiance is described as the HU, the divine breath breathing existence into manifestation. HU is the first exhale of Being, the vibratory impulse by which the unmanifest reveals itself in form. It is not an action but an illumination.

Emergence is that illumination.

But the idealizing object relation bends this illumination through the gaze of the idealized other. Instead of expressing the divine breath directly, the psyche learns to exhale in a shape that will secure approval or belonging. Radiance becomes display—a synthetic shine curated to match the desires of the idealized figure. The peacock is an ideal symbol for ego self: light rearranged into spectacle.

Idealizing does not block emergence; it redirects illumination into performance and display.

Rejecting and Point Six (Recession)

Recession is the inward force of Being—the natural return of experience into depth. In its pure form, recession is absorption, the quiet inhale through which consciousness returns to ground. This inward movement is not withdrawal but intimacy: the softening that allows what arises to be taken fully into presence.

The rejecting object relation interrupts this movement at its origin. The child turns inward for contact and meets tension, misattunement, or emotional unavailability.

The very gesture of reaching into depth encounters disruption. Instead of being received, the inward movement is met with breakage. What should be intimacy becomes uncertainty. What should be absorption becomes caution.

The organism internalizes this as a rule: turning inward is unsafe. The inhale contracts. The psyche begins to brace against the very movement that leads to depth. Vigilance replaces openness—a subtle flinch forms around experience itself.

Here, the basic mechanism of ego becomes visible. The ego rejects not because something external must be refused, but because intimacy threatens dissolution. The now is dangerous because the now has no structure to maintain ego coherence. Recession would reveal the emptiness at the center of identity, so the psyche turns away pre-emptively. The ego avoids the depth that would absorb it.

Rejecting does not stop recession; it armors it. The inhale remains, but tightened, defended, prepared. The movement that was meant to become union is reshaped into vigilance, and the organism learns to meet life by anticipating interruption rather than receiving it.

Frustration and Point Nine (The Field)

The field is the ground of experience—the still openness that holds emergence and recession. In its essential state, the field is sensitive, spacious, receptive, and attuned. It is the quiet sense of already-being-here, the innate contentment and fullness that requires no achievement, no movement, no effort. It is the silent chamber of being, the subtle hum of existence beneath all experience.

The frustrating object relation interrupts this natural ground. The infant turns toward the environment seeking the effortless nourishment that mirrors the intrinsic satisfaction of the field. But the nourishment is inconsistent. Presence comes and goes. Attunement appears and then collapses. The psyche learns that what is essential cannot be reliably met externally. And so, the organism internalizes the impossibility of finding inner fullness through outer responsiveness.

This is the root of frustration: the attempt to secure essential satisfaction, contentment, and peace through external means. When the world fails to deliver the ground that only Being can provide, the system responds by dampening sensitivity. Rather than endure the repeated pain of unmet contact, the organism dims its aliveness before disappointment arrives. Sensitivity is veiled to avoid the sharpness of loss. Presence softens into withdrawal.

Frustration does not block the field; it veils it. The spaciousness remains, but it is wrapped in numbness. The organism no longer trusts that what it longs for—ease, stability, quiet satisfaction—can be met. The field collapses not because vitality is absent, but because vitality has become too costly to feel.

The Triangle as Developmental and Ontological Architecture

These object relations do not sit beside the triangle—they illuminate its distortions. They reveal why the essential dynamisms bend in precisely these ways:

- Emergence becomes performance because the divine illumination is reshaped by idealization.
- Recession becomes vigilance because the inhale is feared.
- The field becomes numb because frustration is suffering at its core.

Thus, the triangle functions simultaneously as an ontological map and a developmental blueprint. It marks the natural forces of consciousness—illumination, dissolution, and the ground that holds them—and the relational shocks that interrupt those forces.

Every type, every fixation, every defensive structure arises as an echo of these three early distortions. The Enneagram is not a description of identity but of how the respiration of Being becomes kinked, constricted, or delayed as it flows into human experience.

The triangle shows how our innate capacity for affect is shaped into three primary egoic emotions, each marking the precise point where a fundamental force of Being is disrupted in early experience.

Primary Emotions

The three primary emotions—shame, fear, and anger—are not properties of the nine types. They are universal fields that arise when one of the three fundamental forces of the inner triangle is interrupted: emergence at Three, recession at Six, and the field at Nine. Every human being participates in all three. Personality simply patterns how each field is handled.

> **Shame** is the contraction of emergence (Point Three) into self-image. **Fear** is the contraction of recession (Point Six) into vigilance. **Anger** contracts the field (Point Nine) into self-boundary reactivity.

Within each emotional family, the same field is distributed across three points in a triadic way: one point over-emphasizes the emotion, one mediates it, and one becomes largely unconscious of it. These are not three different emotions, but three distinct strategies for living with the same emotional tone.

The Anger Triad (Eight, Nine, One)

This triad lives in the instinctive center. Anger here is about disturbance in the ground of being—when reality does not conform to an inner sense of how things should be.

- **Point Eight** over-emphasizes anger. Anger moves quickly to the surface and becomes the primary way of restoring contact and truth. Disruption is met head-on, with force and immediacy.
- **Point One** mediates anger by suppressing and redirecting it. The energy of anger is channeled into control, correction, and "rightness." Outwardly, this appears as tension, irritation, or moral intensity rather than raw anger. The emotion is present, but filtered.
- **Point Nine** is largely unconscious of anger. The organism goes to sleep around conflict and intensity, numbing or diffusing the rising force to preserve inner and outer harmony. Anger tends to surface only indirectly as stubbornness, delay, or quiet resistance.

Same field, three relationships: fully expressed, filtered and managed, or pushed out of awareness.

The Fear Triad (Five, Six, Seven)

This triad lives in the mental center. Fear here is about the stability of inner ground—whether one can safely open inward without being overwhelmed or destabilized.

- **Point Six** over-emphasizes fear. The uncertainty at the core of recession becomes anxiety, questioning, and scanning. Fear is the central signal to be managed, and much of life is organized around anticipating what could go wrong.
- **Point Seven** escapes fear by staying in motion. Fear is translated into plans, options, and reframing. The organism keeps attention moving ahead of fear, turning threat into possibility or distraction, so the raw experience of fear is rarely met directly.
- **Point Five** expends mental energy to minimize fear. The body pulls back, and the mind retreats into distance, clarity, and analysis. Fear is managed by withdrawing from the field of impact altogether. The emotion is present, but buried under detachment and control of input.

Same field, three relationships: intensified, converted into activity, or hidden under distance.

The Shame Triad (Two, Three, Four)

This triad lives in the emotional/relational center. Shame here is about value and visibility—how one's being appears in the gaze of the other.

- **Point Four** over-emphasizes shame. The sense of deficiency, lack, or flaw is felt fully and often sits at the center of identity. The emotional life leans toward the wound to inhabit and understand it.
- **Point Two** mediates shame through giving and relational focus. The feeling of "not enough" is softened by being useful, needed, or necessary to others. Worth is continually negotiated through care and connection, so shame is present but buffered.
- **Point Three** outruns the field of shame through performance, image, and efficiency. Value is secured by looking the part and achieving it. Shame only shows itself when those strategies fail or fall away.

Same field, three relationships: intensified into identity, softened through giving, or covered over by doing.

Why This Matters for the Triangle

Seen this way, the emotional triads are not just psychological groupings. They show how the three primary emotional fields generated by the triangle are distributed and managed through different strategies of embodiment. Shame, fear, and anger each arise from a contraction of one of the three forces. The triads show how that contraction is lived—over-emphasized, mediated, or pushed out of awareness—depending on where one stands in the larger architecture of the system.

The Instincts

Having seen how the three primary object relations correspond to the three points of the inner triangle, we can now turn to another foundational layer of the system's architecture: the instincts.

Just as the object relations reveal the earliest relational distortions of emergence, recession, and the field, the instincts reveal how these same forces express themselves through the living organism. They are not merely behavioral tendencies but the biological currents that carry the organism into the world, into depth, and into continuity of existence.

When understood at this level, the instincts map naturally onto the triangle because each instinct participates in one of the three fundamental movements of Being. They show how consciousness breathes through biology, and how biology, in turn, shapes the possibilities and limits of consciousness.

Point Three: Emergence and the Social Instinct

Emergence is the outward movement of Being, the illumination that reveals itself in the world. The social instinct expresses this same vector at a biological level. Its essential impulse is toward visibility, participation, recognition, belonging, and orientation within the collective field. It is the organism's movement into relationship, the pull to enter the world of others and find one's place among them.

When the idealizing object relation distorts emergence, the social instinct becomes woven into adaptation, performance, and image management. The instinct itself is not the distortion; it simply carries emergence into the relational field. What becomes distorted is the freedom of that emergence. Radiance bends into display. Illumination becomes a curated shine meant to secure approval or safety.

The social instinct at Three is therefore the organism's biological expression of emergence into the field of others.

Point Six: Recession and the Sexual Instinct

Recession is the inward movement of Being, the absorption through which experience dissolves back into its source. The sexual instinct mirrors this movement in the body. Its essential impulse is toward fusion, depth, intensity, and surrender of separateness. It is the instinct that draws the organism toward penetration of experience and intimate contact.

When the rejecting object relation distorts recession, the sexual instinct becomes entangled with fear, ambivalence, or compulsive merging. The inward path becomes unsafe, and the natural dissolving movement is replaced by vigilance or attraction–repulsion patterns. Again, the instinct itself is pure; it is the psychological interface that distorts it. The recoil from absorption is not biological but egoic.

The sexual instinct at Six is therefore the organism's biological expression of recession into depth.

Point Nine: Field and the Self-Preservation Instinct

The field is the ground of Being, the stillness that holds both emergence and recession. The self-preservation instinct arises from this same ground. Its essential impulse is toward continuity, stability, nourishment, and sustaining the organism across time. It roots consciousness in the body and supports the continuity of life.

When the frustrating object relation distorts the field, the self-preservation instinct may retreat into numbness, comfort-seeking, or self-softening to avoid the pain of unmet attunement. The instinct is never dull; it is the narrowing of contact that emerges when safety is unreliable. The biological need for continuity becomes psychological withdrawal.

The self-preservation instinct at Nine is therefore the organism's biological expression of the field of life.

Instincts and the Animal Nature

A central issue with the instincts is their tendency to distort through our animal nature. Instincts arise from biology; they are the organism's inherited strategies for survival, mating, bonding, and protection. Yet human experience does not operate solely within biology.

When instinct meets psychology, the biological becomes personal, and the vital becomes conditioned. Because our psychology is an extension of our biology, the instincts must be understood in both realms: as somatic forces rooted in the organism, and as psychological patterns shaped by early relational experience.

When the instincts operate purely, they express the inherent dynamism of the triangle. When filtered through fear, relational wounds, or egoic strategies, they bend into forms that reflect the animal nature rather than the essential nature. Thus, instinct is never the distortion; it is the biological intelligence that becomes narrowed or exaggerated through the interface with the human psyche.

The Instincts as Forces Within the Breath of Being

Placed within the architecture of the triangle, the instincts reveal themselves as three biological articulations of the same fundamental forces that structure consciousness:

> • The social instinct carries the outward movement of emergence into the communal world.
> • The sexual instinct carries the inward movement of recession into depth and intimacy.
> • The self-preservation instinct carries the grounding movement of the field into continuity and stability.

They do not modify personality; they express how Life enters and moves through the organism. They are biological currents woven into the breath of Being.

Micro-Expressions in Daily Life

Although the three forces of the triangle appear as vast metaphysical movements—illumination, absorption, and the sustaining field—they also reveal themselves continually in the smallest moments of ordinary life. Every thought, reaction, conversation, and breath carries the imprint of 3–6–9. The triangle is not a distant cosmic structure; it is the architecture of experience.

In any moment of expression, the force of emergence can be felt as the impulse to speak, create, reveal, or clarify. It is the outward stretch of consciousness, the sense of something coming forward from within. Even a simple gesture—reaching for a cup, offering an opinion, raising a question—contains a micro-expression of emergence. The psyche moves outward into form.

In any moment of reflection, hesitation, or turning inward, the force of recession appears. This is not withdrawal but absorption: the inward curve of experience as it takes something in. Pausing to consider a comment, feeling the impact of a tone of voice, sensing a shift in the room—these are all instances of recession. Experience folds back toward depth.

And between these movements lies the field, the quiet ground of awareness that holds both expression and absorption. It is present in the silence between words, the stillness before a reaction, the spaciousness that allows a moment to be felt rather than managed. The field is not something we create; it is the background that is always there, stabilizing the movement of emergence and recession.

These micro-expressions reveal that the triangle is the immediate structure of consciousness as it appears in the manifest world. Pure consciousness is unstructured, open, and without differentiation. But the moment consciousness enters form—attention, sensation, relational contact, breath—it takes on a patterned shape.

The triangle marks this shaping. Every shift of attention, every nuance of contact, every inhalation and exhalation reflects the same threefold rhythm through which consciousness becomes experience. Seeing the triangle at the micro-level prepares the ground for understanding the hexad at the macro-level. What unfolds across the entire system is already present in miniature within each lived moment, as consciousness moves from its unformed nature into patterned expression.

The Deep Structure of 3–6–9

Convergence of Forces, Object Relations, Instincts, and Emotions

When the three forces of the triangle are considered alongside the three primary object relations, the three instinctual drives, and the three primary emotions, a single architecture emerges. What usually appears as separate systems—ontological movement, developmental distortion, biological intelligence, and emotional patterning—is revealed to be one unified structure expressing itself through different layers of human experience.

> **At Point Three**, the outward illumination of emergence is shaped through idealizing, expressed biologically through the social instinct, and contracts emotionally into shame. What begins as radiant expression becomes filtered through the gaze of the other.

> **At Point Six**, the inward absorption of recession becomes bent through rejection, expressed biologically through the sexual instinct, and contracts emotionally into fear. What begins as intimacy with depth becomes guarded and vigilant.

> **At Point Nine**, the still openness of the field becomes contracted through frustration, expressed biologically through the self-preservation instinct, and distorts emotionally into anger. What begins as spaciousness becomes reactive when stability is disturbed.

These correspondences are not parallel categories but three lenses on a single dynamic. They reveal how Being emerges, dissolves, and sustains itself through the organism, and how interruptions in these forces generate the core affective tones of human life.

The profundity of the triangle lies in the way these dimensions interlock, making 3–6–9 the foundational coordinates through which the entire enneagramic system reflects life as a process of unfoldment. What looks like psychological structure is, at its root, ontological pressure meeting environmental response.

Energy and Force

A further clarity emerges when the instincts are seen in relation to the triangle and primary emotions: the dynamic forces at 3, 6, and 9 are not energies in themselves. Energy is too narrow and too mechanical a word for what these points express. The triangle describes forces—elemental orientations of being, consciousness, and nature. Energy appears only as the expression of these deeper forces:

- Biologically through instinctual energy
- Developmentally through energetic object relation structures
- Emotionally through the kinetic texture of the field
- Phenomenologically through emergence, recession, and the field.

Energy is what the force produces; it is the visible effect of an invisible orientation.

To call 3–6–9 energies is to mistake the illumination for the light it casts, the inhale for the air it moves, and the field for the sensations that arise within it. What the triangle marks are the forces that generate energies, not the energies themselves.

The Three-Brained Being

Gurdjieff described the human being as a three-brained creature. He wasn't speaking metaphorically or symbolically. He was describing the architecture of human biological presence: three distinct yet interwoven modes of intelligence—head, heart, and belly—each with its own way of knowing, perceiving, and responding.

Modern neuroscience has since verified what ancient wisdom always suggested:

- The cranial brain governs representation, interpretation, and symbolic processing.
- The cardiac nervous system participates in emotional attunement, coherence, and the immediate felt sense of connection.
- The enteric nervous system regulates instinct, orientation, drive, and the visceral foundation of presence.

These three centers form the living field of human intelligence. Each contributes something essential. Each carries its own truth. Each becomes distorted when disconnected from the others.

People who come to the Enneagram through personality typology usually start with this basic structure: there are three centers of intelligence, and these centers appear to be mapped onto the core points of the triangle at 3, 6, and 9. This is the first place where confusion arises, and it is not the reader's fault. In personality teaching:

- 3 is associated with the heart center
- 6 with the head center
- 9 with the belly center

For someone trained only in typology, the assumption seems obvious: the centers must originate at these points. But they do not. The traditional mapping tells us something significant, but it does not tell us where the centers originate. It tells us where each type struggles.

In classical typology:

- Type 3 loses contact with genuine feeling and the felt terrain of the heart.
- Type 6 loses contact with inner guidance, clarity, and the mind's capacity for grounded knowing.
- Type 9 loses contact with instinctual drive and the belly's capacity to assert presence.

These are not locations of intelligence. They are locations of conflict. They show where the thread of connection frays.

So, before going further, it is essential to separate two things that are often conflated. The first is the centers' biological origins.

> **The head center** expresses conceptual and representational intelligence.
> **The heart center** expresses emotional and relational intelligence.
> **The belly center** expresses instinctual and orienting intelligence.

This is not theory. It is physiological, developmental, and experiential. These centers would exist whether or not the Enneagram were ever drawn.

The second is the psychological mapping of typology. The Enneagram assigns the heart, head, and belly centers to points 3, 6, and 9, not to indicate origin, but to show where the personality type breaks connection. The mapping is diagnostic, not anatomical. It identifies the center that a particular type has difficulty accessing or trusting, not the center's source within the organism.

This distinction becomes critical when we begin to work with the Enneagram as living process rather than a typology. To do that, we must introduce another dimension of the symbol that many personality students have never been shown.

Points 3, 6, and 9 also constitute the system's structural triad. They represent the essential rhythm of human psychological movement:

- Outward motion, reactive motion, and settling motion.
    - Three expresses assertion, initiation, and drive.
    - Six expresses counterforce, reactivity, and caution.
    - Nine expresses settling, inertia, and the return to baseline.

This triad describes something completely different from the centers. It explains how any phenomenon moves through the psyche:

- Object relations arise in the head center, but they rush outward at 3, recoil at 6, and dissolve into inertia at 9.
- Emotions arise in the heart center, but they flare outward at 3, contract at 6, and flatten at 9.
- Instincts arise in the belly center, but they surge at 3, brace at 6, and settle at 9.

The structural triad does not describe what something is; it explains how it moves.

Orthogonal Frameworks

A student grounded in typology might feel these two mappings should align.

- **If three** is linked to the heart center, shouldn't emotional phenomena originate at 3?
- **If six** is linked to the head, shouldn't object relations arise there?
- **If nine** is linked to the belly, shouldn't instincts be born at 9?

The answer is no, and here is why: the two triads are describing different dimensions of the same human experience. They are orthogonal frameworks.

An orthogonal framework is a second map that explains a different aspect of the same reality. It does not repeat the first map. It does not contradict the first map. It simply operates on a different axis.

The centers triad and the structural triad are independent dimensions. One describes the origin of intelligence. The other represents the movement of intelligence. The personality mapping adds a third dimension, describing the location of disconnection from intelligence.

Once these layers are separated, everything becomes clear. What appears contradictory is simply multidimensional.

- **The centers triad** tells us where a function originates.
- **The structural triad** tells us how that function behaves.
- **The personality triad** tells us where access to that function becomes compromised.

Each triad reveals something the others do not. Each is necessary for understanding the full complexity of human experience. And none of them cancels out the others.

For a student grounded in personality typology, this can feel like learning that a familiar map was never wrong, only incomplete. The Enneagram was always larger than typology. It was initially a process diagram, a symbol describing transformation, movement, and the unfolding of consciousness. Personality typology is a later development. It is enormously helpful, but it does not stand alone. To work with the Enneagram deeply, these layers must be recognized, not combined into a single simplified picture.

In the context of the three-brained being, the Enneagram becomes a mirror of our structure. Human beings think with the head, feel with the heart, and orient with the belly. These capacities influence each other constantly. The Enneagram reflects this interplay by allowing multiple frameworks to intersect. It shows where a function arises, how it moves, and where it gets lost. This is not confusion. It is completeness. It is the complexity of human nature held in a single symbol.

This chapter establishes the foundation for understanding how personality crystallizes from the interaction of these independent dimensions. What we call a type is not simply a preference or an attitude. It is the result of a deeper process:

- One center becoming dominant
- One movement becoming habitual
- One relationship to a center becoming strained.

When this is understood, the Enneagram stops being a classification system and becomes what it was always intended to be: a living map of human unfolding.

Reframing the Enneagram Through the Lens of Process

The purpose of this book is to widen the aperture through which we understand the Enneagram. Rather than treating the nine personality types as the primary subject, we return to the Gurdjieffian origin: the Enneagram as a process-symbol, a living diagram of forces, movements, interruptions, and transformations. Personality becomes one expression—one crystallization—of deeper dynamisms already at work. By situating the types within the dynamism of the triangle, the object relations, the instincts, and the primary emotions, we reveal a larger architecture.

The Enneagram of Personality Types is not replaced but re-contextualized. It becomes a map of how the organism adapts to these primordial forces, rather than the system's starting point. In this way, we shift from describing patterns to understanding the living process that generates them.

The triangle reveals the three forces that animate all transformation. But these forces do not operate in isolation—they work through a specific pattern of movement, a hidden rhythm that keeps the process alive. This is where we turn to the hexad: the inner figure that shows how energy actually descends through the circle's nine points and returns to its source.

The Hexad

The Hidden Architecture

Inside the outer circle lies a six-pointed figure—the hexad. This inner shape reveals something essential: energy does not move smoothly through time. It leaps, pulses, quickens, and slows. The hexad shows the hidden rhythm beneath every process, the intelligence that keeps life from running mechanically.

If the circle represents the full arc of becoming, the hexad shows the how—the way energy actually behaves as it unfolds. Rather than moving point by point around the rim, the current follows a specific pattern: **1 to 4, then 2, 8, 5, 7, and back to 1**. These jumps are not arbitrary. They follow the same mathematical ratios that shape the musical octave. Just as sound moves in intervals rather than straight lines, consciousness rises and falls in waves throughout the cycle.

The Hexad's Movement

Each inner leap corresponds to a shift in the outer process—a change of direction or density.

> The movement from **1 to 4** represents essence descending into form. Being becomes individuality. The pure impulse of rightness and order (1) encounters itself as self-awareness and depth (4). This is the first great turn—the moment when consciousness recognizes itself as separate from what it observes.

> The jump from **4 to 2** reflects how self-consciousness, once born, seeks connection through love and relationship. Individuality, having awakened to itself (4), reaches outward toward otherness (2). The soul discovers it exists in relationship, not isolation.

> The movement from **2 to 8** grounds that love in embodiment, giving it strength and presence. The outward flow of connection (2) requires power and will to manifest (8). Love must take form, must become concrete, must ground itself in the body and world.

> From **8 to 5**, energy turns inward, power becoming reflection and understanding. The force that just manifested (8) now contemplates what it has created (5). Strength turns to knowledge, embodiment to insight. This is the mind awakening from action.

From **5 to 7**, thought loosens into imagination and freedom. Understanding (5) that has crystallized must now expand toward possibility (7). The mind, having grasped what is, opens to what could be. Constraint gives way to creativity.

Finally, from **7 back to 1**, the current completes its circuit, returning to the original impulse at a higher octave. Imagination and possibility (7) resolve back into order and rightness (1)—but now enriched by the entire journey. The cycle begins again, but at a higher frequency.

These inner shifts continually feed the outer process. They act as energetic infusions that keep the cycle alive. Without them, the circle would be a closed loop—endlessly repeating without renewal. With them, the system breathes. It gains the power to self-correct, to lift itself from habit into consciousness.

How the Triangle Creates the Hexad

But where does this hexadic pattern come from? Why these specific connections and not others? The answer lies in the triangle—the three forces of awareness (9), action (3), and receptivity (6).

The hexad is not separate from the triangle. It is what the triangle generates as the three forces interact with the circle's nine points. When awareness, action, and receptivity move through the field of consciousness, they create this specific six-pointed pattern. The hexad is the visible trace of the triangle's invisible work.

This is the Law of Three meeting the Law of Seven. The three forces must operate for anything to exist or change. The seven-stage process shows how those three forces actually unfold in time.

The Triadic Organization

Before we see how these forces create the hexad's sequential movement, notice their underlying organization. Each of the three forces governs a triad—a group of three points that express its particular quality:

Emergence: 3 → 1 → 4 = The active force manifesting through doing, ordering, and individuating.

Recession: 6 → 2 → 8 = The receptive force internalizing through questioning, connecting, and embodying.

Field: 9 → 5 → 7 = The reconciling force witnessing through awareness, understanding, and imagining.

Placed together, the pattern becomes unmistakable. The nine points are not random variations but three expressions of each fundamental force. This is why understanding the triangle unlocks the entire system—it reveals the organizing principle beneath apparent diversity.

Watch how this unfolds:

- The active force (3) initiates movement.
- That movement meets receptivity (6), which allows it to enter the system.
- Awareness (9) witnesses and reconciles the whole process.
- As these three forces pulse through the nine points of manifestation, they create the 1-4-2-8-5-7 sequence—the natural law of how energy descends into form.

Every point on the hexad requires all three forces to function. Point 1 needs awareness (9) to recognize rightness, action (3) to manifest it, and receptivity (6) to allow it to take form. Point 4 needs all three forces to access authentic depth. Without the triangle, the hexad would be a description without movement. Without the hexad, the triangle would be potential without manifestation.

This is why Gurdjieff called it the Law of Seven: it describes the inevitable pattern that emerges when the Law of Three operates within the field of manifestation. You cannot have one without the other. The triangle provides the forces; the hexad shows the path those forces travel.

The Hexad Types vs. Triangle Types

Understanding this distinction is crucial for anyone coming from personality-type systems:

- The **hexad types** (1, 2, 4, 5, 7, 8) represent the stages of descent and ascent—the journey of consciousness through manifestation. They show what is unfolding as energy moves through time.
- The **triangle types** (3, 6, 9) represent the forces that enable that journey. They show how it unfolds—the three fundamental energies that animate all stages.

The hexad is the river. The triangle is what makes the river flow.

Every point on the hexad requires all three triangle forces to operate. Without awareness (9), action becomes mechanical. Without action (3), nothing manifests. Without receptivity (6), nothing new can enter. The triangle types are not just three more personality patterns—they are the underlying principles that make personality possible in the first place.

This is why triangle types often report feeling less "fixed" than hexad types, or why they can seem harder to type. They're not primarily stages in a process—they're the forces animating all stages.

The Living System

The hexad is the Enneagram's nervous system. It keeps the circle from becoming static. It shows how the process both descends and ascends, revealing that every manifestation contains the potential for renewal. The outer rim traces the story of our lives, but the hexad shows the heartbeat underneath—the continuous conversation between Being and becoming.

During descent, energy moves through the hexad condensing into greater density. Awareness identifies with form. What was flow becomes structure. This is involution—consciousness entering limitation.

During ascent, energy moves through the same pattern but with increasing transparency. Identification loosens. Structure becomes flow again. This is evolution—consciousness recognizing itself within the very pattern that once bound it.

The apparent reversal is not in the direction of energy but in consciousness's relationship to it. The hexad doesn't spin backward; awareness penetrates it more deeply, transforming what was once mechanical repetition into conscious participation.

The triangle provides the forces. The hexad shows how those forces move through time. The circle displays the full spectrum of what those forces create. Together, these three geometries form a complete picture: not just what we are, but how we got here and how we can return.

This is the architecture beneath personality. Once you see it, the Enneagram stops being a typing system and reveals itself as what it always was: a map of how consciousness works.

The Hexad and the Musical Scale

The enneagram can also be understood as a kind of living music. Like a musical scale, it shows how energy rises and falls, expands and contracts, in a rhythm that repeats at every level of life. The ancient idea of the octave—Do, Re, Mi, Fa, So, La, Ti, Do—illustrates this natural law. Each tone represents a step in the unfolding of energy, yet within that sequence, there are two missing semitones, natural pauses that require new input for the process to continue. These correspond to the intervals between Points Three and Four and between Points Six and Seven, the same shock points that appear structurally in the enneagram.

When we translate the points of the enneagram into the language of the octave, a clear correspondence emerges:

- **Point One** is Do, the original impulse of Being, the first clear arising of intention or direction.

- **Point Two** is Re, the responsive movement of attraction and love, energy reaching toward the other.

- **Point Three** is Mi, the expansion into activity and expression, the flowering of initiative and doing.

At this stage, the first shock point appears. In the musical scale, the gap between Mi and Fa cannot be bridged by momentum alone. A new quality must enter. In the enneagram, this is the interval where awareness from Point Nine must enter to keep the process connected to its source. Without this subtle descent of presence from the field, movement hardens into activity cut off from Being.

- **Point Four** is Fa, reflection and individuation, the turning inward of consciousness to feel itself.

- **Point Five** is So, the movement of understanding and synthesis, the mind gathering what experience has revealed.

- **Point Six** is La, the stage of faith or doubt, depending on whether awareness remains present. Here, the structure either opens into trust or tightens into fear.

Between Six and Seven comes the second shock point. In the octave, this is the second semitone gap, where another infusion is required for the progression to continue upward. In the enneagram, this is where a new energy must enter: grace, renewal, or the creative will of Point Three flowing back into the system in a subtler, refined form.

- **Point Seven** is Ti, the transition toward a higher octave, the light, quick, forward-leaning energy that prepares the system to rise.

- **Point Nine**—or the new One—is Do again, the return to unity at a higher vibration, the re-emergence of the field as a more conscious ground.

In this musical view, every process follows the same curve. Energy begins pure, descends into form, meets resistance, renews itself, and returns enriched. The two shock points are where this renewal happens—where consciousness must participate so the cycle can rise rather than merely repeat. Without these infusions, the sequence loops at the same level. With them, the octave ascends.

Within this dynamic, Point Eight occupies a crucial place, even though it does not appear as a discrete tone in the linear presentation of the scale. It represents the phase of embodiment and strength, the moment when renewed energy takes form and becomes real. If the second shock point is the descent of grace, Point Eight is where that grace grounds itself in the world. It is the resonance chamber of the octave, the part of the process that gives power and substance to what has been realized.

Without this phase, insight would remain abstract. Through Point Eight, realization becomes action, spirit becomes body, and understanding becomes lived experience. In the life of personality, Point Eight marks the shift from inner realization to outer presence, the movement from knowing to being, from inspiration to embodiment. Strength here does not mean domination or control; it means fullness—the capacity to stand in one's life with integrity, clarity, and vitality. The energy that began at Point One as a subtle impulse now resonates through the whole system, grounded and audible in reality.

Seen in this way, the enneagram is not only a psychology of types but a symphony of transformation. Every type represents a different melody that has fallen out of tune with the whole. Awareness is what restores harmony. And Point Eight is where that harmony becomes visible and tangible in the world, where the music of Being takes on flesh.

A Historical Note on the Octave and Its Misunderstanding

When Gurdjieff introduced the Law of Seven, he treated it as a central pillar of how reality unfolds. The musical octave was not a metaphor in his teaching but a direct illustration of the rhythm inherent in every process. The two semitone gaps were structural features of the universe, the precise places where a process cannot continue without an infusion of new quality. In this view, the enneagram is not a diagram of character but a diagram of movement—the way energy, consciousness, and experience advance, pause, renew, and ascend.

As the Enneagram entered psychological and popular literature, this foundational layer was often set aside. The octave became a background reference, a curious detail, or a mystical appendix rather than the symbol's engine. Without the Law of Seven as the system's inner motor, the Enneagram easily flattens into a map of personality traits, subtypes, or behavioral tendencies. Nothing in this contemporary use is inherently wrong, yet something essential falls out of view. The dynamism of transformation becomes muted, and the symbol loses its connection to the deeper rhythm Gurdjieff intended to illuminate.

When we restore the octave to its rightful place, the symbol regains its original dimensionality—which is what the next sections will reveal more explicitly.

The Shock Points

Within the Enneagram's circle, two thresholds mark the moments where consciousness either contracts into personality or opens into presence. These lie between Points 3 and 4, and between Points 6 and 7. They are called the shock points—not obstacles to avoid but opportunities for awareness to enter. Every process, whether spiritual or psychological, must pass through them.

These are not ideas. They are lived moments, repeated daily in ways so subtle we rarely notice. They are the pause before you speak, the instant when momentum falters, the gap between what you intended and what actually occurs. At these thresholds, something is needed that effort alone cannot provide.

Between Three and Four

The first shock point is the turn from doing to being—from outward expression to inner awareness. The soul encounters its reflection.

Without awareness, reactivity takes over. The energy that was meant to flow forward bends inward, forming self-image and identification. The soul begins to mistake expression for existence, doing for being. This is where essence becomes self-conscious—where the flow of life, meeting resistance, crystallizes into personality.

Watch a child praised for being good, helpful, or smart. Watch how naturally they begin to repeat what brought approval. The once spontaneous flow becomes strategic—identity forms around what worked. The current, which should continue its journey, circles back.

Presence at this same threshold transforms the process completely. Doing becomes conscious. The soul sees itself acting yet remains unbound by the act. Awareness illuminates experience without claiming it. This is the birth of insight—the first conscious shock—where life turns inward not to contract but to recognize itself.

Between Six and Seven

The second shock point mirrors the first at a higher octave. Through experience, the soul arrives at the edge of renewal. The mind has done all it can. Understanding has reached its limit.

Without awareness, the process collapses into repetition. The flow that should open into freedom turns into anxiety, planning, or escape—the effort to make the next moment different from this one. Energy scatters or freezes. The cycle exhausts itself.

But when awareness enters, AND the active force flows through receptivity, this same point becomes the gateway of grace. Energy that once scattered becomes still (awareness). What was mental exhaustion becomes creative renewal (active force). Fear transforms into faith, and stagnation becomes movement. The soul opens to something finer than thought—not just peaceful allowing, but inspired action, direct knowing, the creative impulse of Being carrying the process forward into Point Seven's imagination and possibility.

At the first shock point, awareness reconnects doing with Being. At the second shock point, both awareness AND creative will enter through the same portal of receptivity—completing what the mind alone could never accomplish.

The Flow of Energy and Awareness

This table summarizes how energy and awareness move through the circle, identifying the location of each shock point.

Phase of Process	Direction of Movement	Essential Activity	Shock Point	If Reactivity Enters	If Awareness Enters
1 → 2 → 3	Outward flow	Being expressing a love and action	Between 3 and 4	Doing becomes identification; self-consciousness begins	Insight arises; doing remains connected to Being
4 → 5 → 6	Inward reflection	Awareness turning toward mind and analysis	Between 6 and 7	Mind tightens; understanding turns into fear or control	Receptivity opens; renewal enters as grace & allowing
7 → 8 → 9 → 1	Return and embodiment	Energy grounds realization and completes the cycle	—	Repetition; personality hardens	Completion; awareness integrates as presence

The Universal Rhythm

Together, these two shock points reveal a universal rhythm: creation, contraction, and conscious renewal. They are not separate events but two faces of one dynamic—the descent of essence into form and its return to source.

- The first shows where the soul forgets. The second shows where it remembers.
- The first bends awareness into self. The second releases self back into awareness.

Every transformation depends on these two entries of consciousness. The first restores contact with Being through recognition. The second completes the cycle through grace. Together they form the hidden mechanism by which the soul evolves—turning interruptions into openings, patterns into paths.

You finish speaking in the meeting and immediately scan faces for reaction. Did it land? Did you sound smart? The words are barely out, and already you're reviewing them, adjusting your image of how you came across. That scanning, that slight tightening in your chest—that's the threshold. Expression just met self-consciousness.

How Personality Forms

Personality begins not as a flaw but as a creative adaptation. The soul's natural flow meets interruption—moments when awareness does not enter—and the movement of Being is forced to find another way forward. But this interruption does not happen in a vacuum. It occurs within a specific architecture, and understanding that architecture reveals why nine distinct patterns emerge rather than an infinite number of variations.

Three Dimensions of Type Formation

Personality does not arise from a single cause. It is not created by one center, one habit, or one emotional pattern—an Enneagram type forms when three independent dimensions of human functioning intersect in a stable, self-reinforcing way. A type is not a preference or a style. It is the crystallization of a deeper structural geometry: origin, movement, and disconnection locking into place.

Every human being is born with three centers of intelligence. These are not optional. They are built into the architecture of our biology.

> **The head** generates imagery, cognition, and meaning.
> **The heart** generates emotional resonance and relational awareness.
> **The belly** generates instinctual orientation, grounding, and energetic mobility.

When these three centers communicate freely, human experience remains fluid, responsive, and adaptable.

But early in life, experience becomes patterned. Emotional overwhelm, relational mismatch, environmental instability, and subtle developmental ruptures influence how each center learns to function. One center may become overdeveloped. Another may remain dormant. A third may drift in and out of contact. These imbalances do not create a type by themselves, but they establish the terrain within which type will eventually crystallize.

The second dimension is the movement pattern of 3, 6, and 9. This movement is not psychological preference; it is the natural rhythm through which all inner phenomena unfold. Some children learn to favor outward motion as a way to engage the world. Others learn to favor reactive motion as protection or scanning.

Still others settle into inertia as a way to maintain safety or reduce overwhelm. This favored movement becomes habitual long before a stable identity emerges. Over time, it shapes how the child approaches effort, expectation, disappointment, and possibility.

The third dimension is the line of disconnection at the core of every personality type. This is not a dysfunction of the centers themselves. It is a break in contact. It is the moment when experience becomes too much or too little, and the child unconsciously decides to stop feeling one center fully. **For type 3**, the heart becomes unsafe. **For type 6**, the head becomes unreliable. **For type 9**, the belly becomes overwhelming. This disconnection occurs not as a choice but as an adaptation. It protects the young psyche in the moment but creates a long-term structural imbalance.

When the Interruption Occurs

Now watch how these three dimensions converge at the shock points—the specific thresholds where the flow of Being encounters its natural pause.

At the **first shock point**, between Points 3 and 4, spontaneous expression encounters an environment that cannot fully receive it. The child feels something break in the current. Without the capacity for conscious awareness, the soul interprets this not as a pause in the flow but as emotional and energetic evidence: *something is wrong with me.*

A child shows their drawing—proud, open, offering it freely. The parent glances up, distracted: "That's nice, honey." The light in the child's eyes dims almost imperceptibly. They look at the drawing again, differently now. What was offering becomes checking: Is it good enough? That dimming, that checking—that's where the flow bent inward.

The energy of aliveness folds back upon itself. What was once effortless becomes effort. Expression becomes performance. Curiosity becomes caution. The soul learns to adapt, to compromise, to manage the flow rather than trust it.

In this moment, the three dimensions begin to lock together:

- The dominant center leads in managing this adaptation.
- The favored movement pattern—outward assertion (3), reactive caution (6), or settling withdrawal (9)—becomes the primary strategy for handling the interruption.
- The disconnection begins to form: the heart goes offline for some types, the head for others, the belly for still others.

What the child cannot feel, cannot trust, or cannot access becomes the invisible scaffolding around which identity organizes itself.

At the **second shock point**, between Points 6 and 7, the pattern deepens. The strategies formed at the first threshold no longer guarantee safety or connection. Fear, uncertainty, or the pressure to maintain an image begins to dominate. What could have been renewal—surrender into trust—becomes a search for control, stimulation, or reassurance. The soul learns to survive through repetition rather than presence.

By this point, the type structure has crystallized. The dominant center continues to take precedence. The habitual movement repeats in familiar situations. The disconnection silently shapes what the person can feel, know, and act upon. The configuration becomes increasingly stable—not because it is permanent, but because it has become the most reliable pattern for navigating the world.

The Nine Ways the Flow Bends

Each of the nine types forms around the memory of these interruptions—a specific moment when the stream of essence was diverted into survival. The qualities of Being remain, but their expression narrows. Love turns into need. Strength into control. Intelligence into judgment. Joy into restlessness.

The child, unable to rest in Being, identifies with one aspect of experience and builds a world around it. These adaptive structures keep life going when presence falters, but they also veil the direct knowing of what we are.

> **Point One** – The loss of inherent perfection leads to striving for it. The soul confuses divine order with personal control, mistaking effort for purity.

> **Point Two** – The loss of essential love gives rise to the need to earn it. The soul learns to meet others' needs as a way to feel connected to its heart.

Point Three – The loss of effortless radiance becomes identification with performance. The soul turns Being into doing, equating worth with success.

Point Four – The loss of direct contact with depth becomes a search for uniqueness. The soul makes an identity out of longing, seeking what it already is.

Point Five – The loss of innate knowing becomes detachment into observation. The soul withdraws into thought, mistaking conceptual understanding for safety.

Point Six – The loss of trust in Being becomes dependence on external certainty. The soul replaces inner faith with vigilance and allegiance to structures.

Point Seven – The loss of natural joy turns into the pursuit of stimulation. The soul resists limitation, chasing variety to avoid the emptiness of disconnection.

Point Eight – The loss of essential strength becomes control through force. The soul hardens into assertion, protecting vulnerability by dominating experience.

Point Nine – The loss of effortless unity becomes avoidance of conflict. The soul withdraws into inertia, mistaking comfort for peace.

From this perspective, the Enneagram of personality is a map of nine ways the soul continues its journey after losing immediate contact with essence. Each type reveals how the flow bent inward at the first shock point and sought stability before the second. These patterns are ingenious, not mistaken. They are the soul's attempt to remember its source by recreating it.

The Crystallization

By adolescence, the type structure is usually solidified. A type has formed when these three dimensions align:

- The dominant center takes the lead.
- The favored movement pattern becomes the primary strategy.
- The disconnection becomes the invisible scaffolding around which identity organizes itself.

These three layers reinforce each other until personality feels natural, inevitable, and even necessary. The child does not experience this as a structure. The child experiences it as themselves and the world.

What was once a creative adaptation eventually becomes automatic, a mechanical living. The movement that began as protection becomes a form of inhabited defense. The same pattern repeats because the original interruption was never consciously met. The type becomes a closed loop, endlessly repeating the same gestures because the original flow of renewal was interrupted.

Why This Matters

Recognizing how a type forms reveals why the Enneagram of process is essential for understanding the Enneagram of personality. Each type is not simply a cluster of traits. It is an intersection of three forces:

1. The origin of intelligence (which center)
2. The movement of intelligence (which structural pattern)
3. The break in connection with intelligence (which disconnection).

This is why type descriptions alone cannot transform anyone. They describe the result, not the underlying dynamics.

Personality is not a mistake. It is an intelligent improvisation by consciousness—a necessary structure that allows life to continue under conditions of separation. The problem is not that we have a personality. The problem is that we mistake it for who we are.

The Pathway of Transformation

Transformation begins when these three dimensions are disentangled and seen clearly. The work of liberation is not to change the type. It is to restore the natural flow among the three centers, to loosen habitual movement patterns, and to reestablish contact with the disconnected center. When these three strands begin to reconnect, type loosens. Identity becomes more spacious. Experience becomes more fluid. The person starts to respond from presence rather than pattern.

But the exact mechanism that produced adaptation can become the means of transformation. When awareness touches the automatic pattern, the system begins to open again. In childhood, these thresholds arrived without the capacity for self-reflection. The young soul met the shock points through instinctive reactivity—tightening, withdrawing, performing, or imagining safety elsewhere. Later in life, these same thresholds reappear—not as memories but as living dynamics within experience. They are the points at which awareness can now enter. The soul's movement was never broken; it has simply awaited recognition.

Having seen how type forms, we can now address a widespread misunderstanding about the Enneagram's inner lines. These arrows do not show a person moving from one type to another. They reveal how the field of consciousness draws different qualities into itself—contracting defensively under stress, opening to essential resources under presence. The pattern doesn't travel—the field shifts.

The Meaning of the Arrows

The lines connecting the points of the Enneagram have often been interpreted as paths of integration and disintegration, as though a person literally moves from one type to another. But the arrows do not mark movement through space. They reveal resonance within a single field.

Each point represents a living frequency of consciousness. When awareness contracts, it pulls other frequencies into itself as defenses. When awareness opens, it draws in those same qualities as support and richness. The energy of the system never reverses—it only changes tone according to the depth of presence within it.

What appears as movement along an arrow is really the psyche drawing on the resources of another point in response to how experience is being met. Under reactivity, the pull is a defensive contraction. Under presence, it is integrative expansion. The arrows indicate lines of communication between aspects of the soul, showing how energy can either distort or harmonize depending on the state of consciousness.

Strength Meeting Vulnerability

Take Point Eight as an example. When relaxed and open, the Eight's strength and vitality are grounded in immediacy—body and heart unified in direct contact with reality. Power flows through feeling. The instinct to protect includes the capacity to be touched.

But when the Eight meets threat or emotional intensity, the same life force begins to retreat from the heart. The instinct to stay strong becomes an instinct to stay safe. Feeling, which once grounded power, now seems dangerous.

At that moment, the Eight does not "go to Five." Instead, through reactivity and the need for greater defense, it draws the energy of Five into itself. The Eight's grounded knowing becomes cerebral knowing. Power turns into observation. The vitality that once moved through the body withdraws into the head, seeking safety in distance, analysis, or strategy. This is not travel but dissociation—the energy evacuates feeling and reconstitutes itself as thought.

From the outside, it appears to be a downward shift, but the process's current remains the same. The flow from 2 to 8 to 5 remains part of the hexad's natural rhythm; what changes is the presence within it. Without awareness, the channel narrows, and vitality becomes tension. The heart is silenced so the mind can control what the body once trusted.

When presence returns, something different happens along the same line. The Eight no longer seeks safety through withdrawal but allows strength to include vulnerability. The body relaxes. The heart reopens. In this state, the Eight draws in the receptive warmth of Point Two—not by moving to it but by allowing its quality to resonate within. The same power that once defended against feeling now protects feeling. Strength and tenderness merge.

This is the real meaning of the arrows: they show how the soul breathes. Under reactivity, each type contracts and pulls in what will fortify its separation. Under presence, the same type expands and includes what will restore its wholeness. The arrows are not paths of escape but channels of correspondence through which awareness learns to inhabit itself more fully.

We could say that personality pulls; essence allows. One tightens the field; the other opens it. Every point has these two possibilities. What we call disintegration is simply reactivity, narrowing the flow. What we call integration is presence returning to it. The arrows are not instructions for movement but reminders of relationship—the living threads of resonance that weave the soul back into the whole.

The Hexad Lines in Practice

The hexad is not decoration. It reveals something specific about how energy moves through the system—and more importantly, how your particular type draws on other qualities when presence is lost or regained.

The hexad lines represent the *energetic pathway of transformation*—the specific routes through which consciousness either contracts into deeper defense or expands into greater wholeness.

Why these specific lines? Because they follow the Law of Seven, the mathematical rhythm that governs how energy actually descends into manifestation and ascends back to source. These are not arbitrary connections but the natural currents along which consciousness flows when it enters time.

Let's see how this operates in types beyond Eight.

Love Meeting Force

The Two's line follows: **2 → 8 → 5 → 7 → 1 → 4 → 2**

When the Two is relaxed and present, love flows naturally. The heart is open, generous without agenda, attuned to others without losing itself. There's a quality of ease in giving—it doesn't require anything in return.

But when the Two meets rejection or feels its love is unwanted, something shifts. The open heart doesn't collapse into sadness. Instead, it draws the energy of Point Eight into itself.

Watch what happens: The Two who was just warm and available suddenly becomes forceful, insistent, demanding. "After all I've done for you." The giving that was once soft becomes hard. There's an edge now, a pushing energy. The Two tries to control the connection it fears losing. Love becomes leverage. The heart armors itself with will.

This is not the Two becoming an Eight. This is the Two's field contracting and pulling Eight's defensive posture inward. When love feels rejected, it tries to force recognition. The vulnerability of care transforms into the aggression of demand.

If reactivity continues, the Two can draw even further along the hexad into Point Five's energy. Now the forceful demand gives way to cold withdrawal. "Fine. I don't need you either." The Two who was just pushing suddenly pulls back entirely. The heart closes. Emotional connection is severed. The Two retreats into a defended position, analyzing what went wrong, creating distance where there was once warmth.

But under presence, the same hexad lines reveal something entirely different. When the Two relaxes its need to be needed, it naturally opens to Point Four's essential quality: authentic depth and emotional truth. The heart stops performing love and allows itself to feel without agenda. There's room for genuine sadness, for beauty, for the full range of feeling without it becoming strategy. The Two discovers that real connection includes vulnerability, not just giving.

As presence deepens, the Two can access the qualities that flow through the hexad in their essential form—Eight's true strength that protects without controlling, Five's clarity that observes without withdrawing. The compulsive giving relaxes into natural generosity that includes healthy boundaries and genuine discernment.

Why this particular line? Because Eight's strength and Four's depth are what the Two's love needs to become whole. Without Eight's grounding, love becomes boundaryless and depleting. Without Four's authenticity, love remains strategic rather than real. The hexad shows the natural intelligence of how the soul seeks what it's missing.

Knowing Meeting Participation

The Five's line follows: **5 → 7 → 1 → 4 → 2 → 8 → 5**

When the Five is at ease, knowledge flows naturally. Understanding arises without strain. The mind is spacious, curious, engaged with life rather than observing it from distance. There's a quiet joy in simply knowing.

But when the Five feels intruded upon or overwhelmed by demands, it retreats. The open mind becomes defended. Here, the Five draws Point Seven's energy into itself—but in its reactive form.

The withdrawal doesn't look like stillness; it looks like mental activity. The Five begins spinning out scenarios, possibilities, escape routes. "What if I just..." The mind becomes restless, scattered, seeking freedom through imagination rather than through presence. The quiet observer becomes the anxious strategist.

This is the Five using Seven's mental energy defensively—not to embrace life's possibilities but to avoid its demands. The detachment that once felt wise now feels brittle.

If reactivity intensifies, the Five can pull further into Point One's defensive pattern. The scattered thinking of Seven crystallizes into rigid positions. "I have a system for this." The openness of inquiry hardens into conviction. The Five begins organizing its withdrawal into principles, creating elaborate internal structures that justify not participating.

But when presence returns, the same hexad opens in a different way. The Five, instead of using Seven to escape, opens to Seven's essential quality: delight in the abundance of existence. Knowledge becomes playful rather than protective. The mind that was hoarding becomes generous. Understanding wants to *share* itself, to participate in the world rather than catalog it.

As awareness deepens, the Five touches Point One's essential quality: the rightness of things as they are. Knowledge no longer needs to be complete before the Five engages. There's a trust in the natural order, a sense that participation itself is intelligence. The Five discovers that understanding deepens through involvement, not withdrawal.

Why this particular line? Because Seven's engagement and One's trust are what the Five's knowing needs to rejoin life. Without Seven, knowledge remains isolated. Without One, understanding lacks confidence. The hexad reveals the path from observation to participation.

The Pattern Across All Hexad Types

What becomes clear through these examples:

- The hexad lines are **bidirectional**. They show both how the type contracts (pulling defensive qualities inward) and how it expands (opening to essential qualities). The same pathway that leads into deeper defense, when met with awareness, becomes the route back to wholeness.

- The connections follow **energetic logic**, not personality similarity. Two and Four don't resemble each other superficially, but Four's depth is precisely what Two's love needs. Five and Seven appear opposite, but Seven's engagement is exactly what Five's knowledge requires.

- The hexad shows **the architecture of transformation**. These aren't random associations but the actual circuitry through which consciousness moves as it descends into form and ascends back to source. Understanding your hexad line tells you where to look when the pattern tightens—and what essential qualities want to emerge when it releases.

Practical Recognition

- **For Type Two:** Notice when your giving suddenly feels personal and painful—that's Four's energy being drawn in defensively. Notice when that pain hardens into "they should have"—that's One entering. Can you feel these shifts happening?

- **For Type Five:** Notice when your careful thinking becomes frantic possibility-spinning—that's Seven's energy being used for escape. Notice when that spinning crystallizes into rigid systems—that's One entering. Can you catch the moment of contraction?

- **For all hexad types (1, 2, 4, 5, 7, 8):** Your specific line shows both your path into deeper defense and your way back to essence. The same connections that trap can liberate. Awareness transforms the circuit from a cage into a current.

Understanding the Layers

Type Eight as Field

What follows examines three types in depth - Eight, Four, and Six - representing body, heart, and head centers. The Eight receives particular attention as it's the author's pattern, allowing for the precision that comes from direct observation rather than inference. The same field structure operates for all nine types.

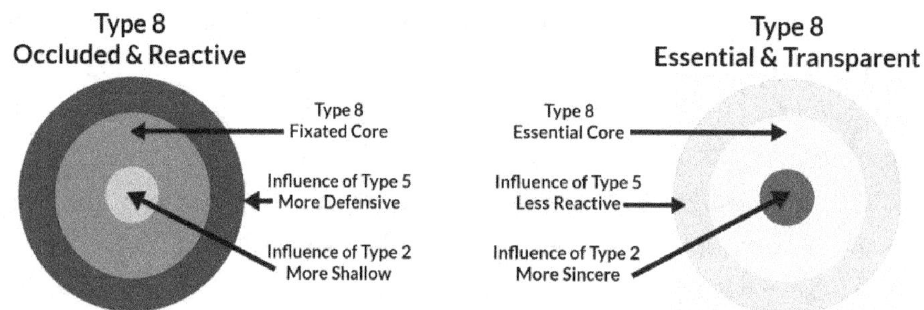

These images illustrate a fundamental aspect of how personality operates. They do not show movement from one type to another, nor do they describe developmental stages. Instead, they reveal how different qualities of consciousness exist simultaneously within a single field, appearing either distorted or clarified depending on the level of awareness.

Both diagrams use concentric circles. Each circle represents a quality that becomes active within the Eight's inner world. What changes is not which qualities are present, but whether they show up occluded by reactivity or transparent to essence.

The Reactive Field

In the occluded state, three distortions appear:

- **The inner ring** shows essential strength compressed into frustration and anger. When contact with Being is lost, strength becomes force—pushing against life, demanding impact, defending against vulnerability.
- **The outer ring** reveals the defensive echo of Point Five. Under pressure, the Eight adopts a posture of withdrawal. The body pulls back. The heart closes. Emotion becomes dangerous, so the Eight retreats into strategy, observation, and distance.

- **The center** reflects the distortion of Point Two's relational impulse. When connection feels unsafe, the Eight may care in ways that protect rather than reveal—offering strength instead of softness, help instead of openness, generosity that maintains control rather than intimacy.

All three distortions occur in the same field. They are layers of one reactive structure, not movements across the Enneagram. The personality is not traveling; the field is contracting.

The Essential Field

In the transparent state, the same three layers appear without distortion:

- **The inner ring** shows essential strength—direct, alive, grounded, unforced. It protects without aggression and acts without domination.
- **The outer ring** reveals Point Five's essential clarity. Not withdrawal, but spaciousness. The mind becomes open, quiet, and receptive. The Eight has room inside. There is both strength and stillness.
- **The center** reflects the essential warmth of Point Two: generosity without strategy, affection without control, connection without fear. This is the heart's natural offering, rooted in presence rather than need.

Type Six as Field

The Six occupies a unique position in the Enneagram—it is the portal through which energy enters at both shock points. Understanding how the Six's field operates illuminates not just one type but the whole mechanism of transformation.

The Reactive Field

In the occluded state, three distortions appear:

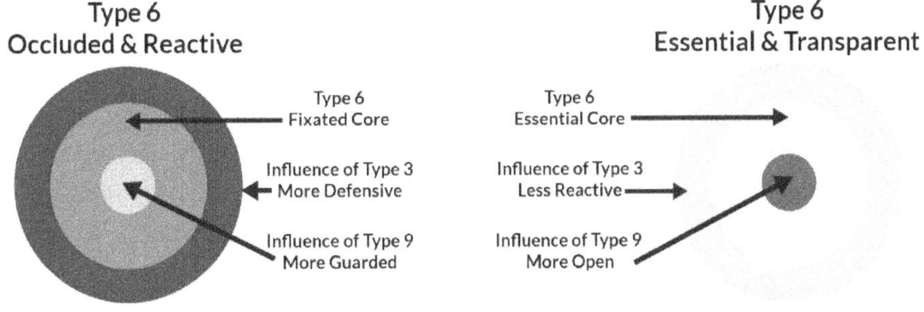

The inner ring shows essential faith compressed into vigilance and doubt. When contact with Being is lost, trust becomes impossible. The Six scans constantly for threat, testing loyalty, questioning everything. What should be natural confidence becomes anxious preparation. The mind races through scenarios, seeking safety in prediction.

The outer ring reveals the defensive echo of Point Three. Under pressure, the Six doesn't rest in uncertainty—it performs confidence. There's a driven quality, an overcompensation. The Six becomes the super-competent one, the hyper-responsible one, the one who can handle it all. But beneath the performance is terror. The doing is compulsive, not creative. Activity becomes a defense against fear.

The center reflects the distortion of Point Nine's capacity for peace. When anxiety becomes unbearable, the Six numbs. Not through direct avoidance like the Nine, but through mental fog or emotional shutdown. The vigilant mind suddenly can't think clearly. Decision becomes impossible. The Six freezes, merging with whatever authority or group offers safety. Self-trust vanishes into compliance.

All three distortions pulse through the same field. The Six oscillates between hyper-vigilance (outer), compulsive action (middle), and frozen compliance (inner), depending on the intensity of threat.

The Essential Field

In the transparent state, the same three layers appear without distortion:

- **The inner ring** shows essential faith—the direct knowing that Being is trustworthy. Not belief, but immediate recognition. The Six rests in uncertainty without needing to resolve it. Questions arise from curiosity rather than fear. There's a quality of courage that neither denies danger nor contracts around it.

- **The outer ring** reveals Point Three's essential quality: authentic effectiveness and natural productivity. Action arises from presence rather than anxiety. The Six discovers it can create, accomplish, and move through the world with grace. Doing becomes an expression of vitality rather than a defense against collapse.

- **The center** reflects Point Nine's essential peace: the stillness that holds all movement. The Six finds it can rest even while engaged, that peace doesn't require the absence of conflict. There's trust in the natural unfolding of things. The need to control the outcome releases.

The Pattern in Six

The Six's contraction follows:

> Loss of inner ground → questioning becomes compulsive → vigilance intensifies → forced competence or frozen compliance → exhaustion.

The Six's expansion reverses this:

> Presence returns → doubt becomes inquiry → faith emerges naturally → action flows from ground → peace holds it all.

What's essential to recognize:

- The Six is the portal precisely because its journey is everyone's journey.
- Every type must move from fear to trust, from mental effort to grace.
- The Six lives this threshold consciously.
- When the Six learns to remain open at the edge of uncertainty, it demonstrates the possibility for all types.

Why Six is the Gateway

At the first shock point (3–4), awareness from Point Nine must enter through the receptivity of Point Six. This is the movement from doing to being, from expression to reflection.

The Six's capacity to question—to not take appearance as reality—is what allows this threshold to become conscious. Without Six's doubt, the Three would never pause to reflect. Without Six's willingness to not-know, awareness couldn't enter.

At the second shock point (6–7), creative energy from Point Three must enter through Six's opening. This is the movement from mental effort to grace. The Six's capacity to *stop insisting*—to release the need to figure it out—is what allows renewal. Without Six's surrender, the mind would exhaust itself. Without Six's trust, grace couldn't flow in.

The Six is not weak or fearful by nature. The Six is the *conscious threshold*—the place where the soul learns to receive what cannot be produced by effort alone.

The Pattern Across All Types

This same field structure operates for every type. Each carries all nine points within itself as potential qualities of consciousness. Some become overdeveloped, some hidden, some defensive—but none are absent.

When awareness deepens, the boundaries between types soften, and the original wholeness reappears. What were separate traits become nine facets of one field of consciousness, each waiting to be reclaimed.

The Dynamics of Descent and Ascent

When energy moves from 1 to 4, and onward through 2, 8, 5, and 7, it follows the inner hexad of the Enneagram—the pattern known as the Law of Seven. This is not energy moving outward around the rim of the circle, which represents the total field of Being, but inward into manifestation. It is the path of involution, the soul's descent into form.

From this perspective, what is often called the direction of disintegration is not moral or psychological failure but simply the movement of energy into greater density. The soul enters limitation, individuality, and experience. Awareness begins to identify with the forms it inhabits, and what was initially flow becomes structure. Personality, in this sense, is condensed consciousness—Being slowed down by its own gravity.

At the two shock points, this energy can either continue condensing through reactivity or begin to transform through presence. The first shock point marks the birth of individuality. The second marks the possibility of renewal. Between them lies the entire range of human development: the soul's journey through experience and its gradual awakening within the very pattern that once bound it.

As awareness awakens, energy doesn't reverse direction—it changes orientation. It begins to move through the same geometry but with increasing transparency. The Enneagram is not a wheel that spins backward; it is a spiral that turns upward through the same pattern. What once served separation now becomes the pathway of integration.

During descent, attention flows outward—into doing, creating, expressing, defining. During ascent, attention flows inward—into being, receiving, unifying. The motion is identical; the awareness inhabiting it is different. The apparent reversal is not in the energy, but in the vector of consciousness.

In personality language, this is what has been misinterpreted as the "direction of integration." An Eight under presence does not travel to Two. Instead, as its defenses soften, it opens to and absorbs the resonance of Point Two—allowing love, tenderness, and attunement to infuse its strength. The energy of Eight doesn't move; its field becomes permeable. The qualities of Two are incorporated into its experience.

As this continues, the Eight–Two field can expand to include Four, bringing emotional depth and authenticity. The same process unfolds for every type. Each point gradually opens to the harmonics it once resisted, integrating them not as opposites but as long-forgotten parts of itself. This is the true ascent: the transformation of division into resonance.

When all points of the circle become transparent to one another, the pattern itself dissolves. The Enneagram no longer describes movement between types, but the return of the circle to wholeness—Being recognizing its geometry from within time.

The Synthesis of the Nine Currents

The nine types are not nine separate personalities but nine variations of one living process. Each reveals how the same current of Being encounters interruption and invents a way to keep moving when awareness does not enter.

The first shock point bends the flow inward; the second offers the opportunity for its return. Between these two thresholds, the soul improvises its particular dance—each type a unique rhythm of the same music.

- **The One** strives to restore divine order.
- **The Two** reaches out to recover love.
- **The Three** performs to re-create radiance.
- **The Four** feels deeply to regain intimacy.
- **The Five** withdraws to preserve clarity.
- **The Six** questions to rebuild trust.
- **The Seven** escapes to rediscover joy.
- **The Eight** controls to reclaim power.
- **The Nine** forgets to remember peace.

All are echoes of the same event: the shock of separation and the longing for reunion. Personality, in every form, is the soul's creative attempt to bridge the distance between essence and experience. Yet within each type, the very movement that sustains separation also conceals the path of return.

When awareness enters—when we consciously meet the same shock points—the circle completes itself. What was once reactivity becomes revelation. The pattern that bound us becomes the map that frees us.

The Enneagram, viewed in this way, is not a description of nine kinds of people, but nine ways Being rediscovers itself over time.

Stages of Awakening Through the Pattern

Understanding the Enneagram intellectually is one thing. Living its liberation is another. Between concept and realization lies a journey with recognizable stages—not a linear progression but a deepening spiral, where each return reveals more of what was always present.

These stages are not achievements to check off, but qualities of relationship with the pattern itself. We don't move through them once; we spiral through them again and again, at deeper levels, as awareness penetrates the structure of personality more fully.

- **Stage One**

  Unconscious Identification - Initially, we are the pattern. There's no distance, no recognition, no choice. The reaction happens, and we believe it. The thought arises, and we take it as truth. The emotion moves through, and we are convinced it defines us.

  Type One believes the inner critic speaks the truth. The Type Four believes the longing means something is actually missing. The Type Eight believes vulnerability equals weakness. The pattern runs automatically, invisibly, shaping every perception.

  At this stage, the Enneagram—if we encounter it—feels flattering or threatening. We either love seeing ourselves described ("Finally, someone understands me!") or resist the description ("That's not really me"). Either way, type becomes identity. We're still inside the pattern, now with a label for it.

- **Stage Two**

  Intellectual Recognition - Eventually, something creates distance. Maybe suffering intensifies. Perhaps a moment of grace reveals a gap between stimulus and reaction. Maybe we read something that lands differently.

  We begin to see the pattern operating. We notice the Type Two reaching out when hurt. We catch the Type Seven escaping when limitations appear. We recognize the Type Six's mind tightening around uncertainty. The pattern is still happening, but now there's observation alongside it.

  This stage often feels exciting—"Aha! That's what I do!" There's relief in naming what was previously invisible. But the pattern hasn't changed. We see it more clearly, but we're still enacting it. The One still judges. The Four still longs. The Eight still controls. Now we know we're doing it.

  The danger here is mistaking recognition for transformation. We can become experts at analyzing our patterns while remaining completely identified with them. The Enneagram becomes a sophisticated story about why we are the way we are, rather than a doorway through it.

• Stage Three

Witnessing the Contraction - Something shifts when we learn to catch the pattern closer to its arising. Not just in reflection—"Oh, I did that thing again"—but in the moment of contraction itself.

You're in conversation and notice the split second when self-consciousness enters. You're about to speak and feel the Three gathering itself into image. You're alone and sense the Four's mood crystallizing into identity. You're asked a question and watch the Five's mind retreat into analysis.

This is the first conscious shock beginning to operate. You're no longer just seeing the pattern in retrospect; you're present at the threshold where it forms. There's awareness before, during, and after the contraction.

The pattern still happens—that doesn't stop. But the identification loosens. You feel yourself performing, but know you're not the performance. You watch the mood arise but recognize it as weather, not self. The contraction occurs in awareness rather than as awareness.

This stage can be uncomfortable. You see the pattern clearly enough that it no longer fully satisfies, but not clearly enough that it dissolves. You're caught between identification and freedom, neither fully inside the pattern nor free of it. The old strategy still activates, but it doesn't convince you the way it used to.

You're about to respond to a criticism and catch yourself gathering a defense. The familiar shape of it, the trajectory of what you were about to say—all of it visible now before it fully forms. You feel the impulse, see the pattern, and for once, there's space around it. The defense might still speak, but you're no longer convinced by it. That space is where freedom lives.

- ## Stage Four

Seeing the Essential Quality Underneath - At some point—and this often comes in glimpses rather than as a permanent state—you begin to sense what the pattern is protecting. Beneath the One's judgment is a love of rightness. Beneath the Four's longing is a capacity for depth. Beneath the Eight's control is tremendous vitality.

The personality is revealed not as a mistake but as a distortion. The essential quality was always there, just compressed through reactivity. The anger is contracted strength. The longing is deflected love. The vigilance is interrupted faith.

When you touch this layer, something profound shifts. The pattern stops being the enemy. You see it as the soul's intelligent, if misguided, attempt to preserve what matters most. Compassion arises—not as a concept but as direct recognition. This is what was trying to survive.

The work at this stage becomes gentler. Instead of fighting the pattern or trying to transcend it, you begin to inquire into what it's protecting. What would happen if you let the One's judgment soften? Not suppress it, but let it reveal the love of order underneath? What if the Four's longing could feel all the way through itself and discover what it's actually seeking?

- ## Stage Five

Essential Qualities Emerging - As the pattern is seen and felt through repeatedly, something unexpected happens: qualities that have nothing to do with personality begin to emerge naturally.

The One discovers spontaneous rightness without having to create it. Things are okay as they are, even imperfect things. The Three finds authentic presence without performance. Being replaces doing as the source of realness. The Six rests in trust that isn't belief—just immediate knowing that Being is reliable.

These aren't achievements or spiritual states you've attained. They're what was always here, no longer obscured by the pattern's tightness. The personality hasn't disappeared; it's become transparent. You can feel its movement, but you're no longer convinced by it.

This stage often brings unexpected ordinariness. There's less drama, less intensity, less sense of "me" navigating through life. The One no longer needs to be the conscious one. The Four stops needing to be the deep one. The Eight stops needing to be the strong one. Life moves, and you move with it.

- **Stage Six**

    Living From Essence - Eventually—and this deepens over years, not weeks—presence becomes the ground rather than the exception. The pattern still arises in moments of stress or unconsciousness, but it no longer defines experience. You know yourself as awareness, not as the pattern awareness occasionally illuminates.

    At this stage, the type becomes something you *do* sometimes rather than what you *are*. The Three might still feel the pull toward performance in specific contexts, but it's recognized immediately as a movement within consciousness rather than as truth. The Six might still feel uncertainty, but there's no collapse into it. The pattern is seen as a pattern, and life continues.

    What's most striking here is that the essential qualities don't feel special or elevated. The One's rightness, the Two's love, the Eight's strength—these are how life expresses itself through this particular nervous system. There's nothing to maintain, nothing to achieve, nowhere else to be.

    At this stage, the Enneagram is no longer a map of who you are. It's a reminder of how consciousness can contract, and how presence reveals what was never lost. You might reference it occasionally when you notice contraction happening, but mostly you're just living. The symbol has done its work.

The Spiral Nature of the Journey

These stages don't unfold linearly. You may experience the essential qualities of Stage Five briefly, then find yourself back in Stage Two's intellectual analysis. You might witness the contraction clearly (Stage Three) in one area of life while remaining unconsciously identified (Stage One) in another.

The journey spirals. Each time you return to a stage, you meet it with greater awareness, greater capacity, and more space. What was once a months-long unconscious identification might become a minutes-long contraction you catch quickly. What once required intense effort to witness becomes effortless recognition.

The key insight: transformation isn't about getting somewhere else. It's about inhabiting where you are with increasing consciousness. The personality doesn't need to be eliminated; it needs to be seen. The pattern doesn't need to be transcended; it needs to be recognized as a pattern.

This is the gift of the Enneagram when understood as a living process rather than a fixed type: it shows both the architecture of how we forgot and the pathway through which we remember.

Shock Points in Living Moments

Understanding how the soul's flow becomes interrupted is one thing. Catching the moment of interruption as it happens is another entirely. The shock points are not theoretical constructs to be believed in; they are lived thresholds we cross dozens of times each day, usually without noticing.

What follows are not techniques but invitations to recognition—ways of sensing when the flow encounters its natural pause and what happens in that instant before awareness enters or reactivity takes over.

The Felt Sense of the First Shock Point

You're moving through your day with a certain momentum. Energy is flowing outward—you're engaged, creating, expressing, handling what needs handling. Then something happens.

Maybe it's a glance from someone that lands wrong. A comment in a meeting. An email that shifts the atmosphere. Your own reflection caught unexpectedly in a window.

In that instant, something changes. The outward flow turns inward. You become aware of yourself being seen, being evaluated, being someone rather than simply doing what you're doing.

This is the threshold between Three and Four. This is where expression meets self-consciousness—and where the superego is born.

The superego is what perches at this threshold.

It's the internal judge, the watcher, the voice that evaluates everything you do before you do it. When awareness fails to enter consciously at the 3-4 shock point, this structure forms as a substitute for presence and objective consciousness. Instead of consciousness witnessing experience, the superego evaluates it. Instead of awareness illuminating action, the judge measures it against an internalized standard.

Each type's superego takes a different shape based on what was lost:

- **The One's superego says:** "You're not good enough. You must be better."
- **The Two's superego says:** "You're not loving enough. You must give more."
- **The Three's superego says:** "You're not successful enough. You must achieve more."
- **The Four's superego says:** "You're not special enough. Something is missing."
- **The Five's superego says:** "You don't know enough. You must understand more."
- **The Six's superego says:** "You're not safe enough. You must be more prepared."
- **The Seven's superego says:** "This isn't enough. There must be something better."
- **The Eight's superego says:** "You're not strong enough. You must not be weak."
- **The Nine's superego says:** "Don't assert yourself. Keep the peace."

The superego masquerades as helpful—as the voice keeping you on track, protecting you from shame, ensuring you don't fail. But it's actually the mechanism of separation. It sits at the threshold where doing should flow naturally into being, and instead creates a split: the doer and the watcher, the actor and the critic,

What it feels like:

- A sudden awareness of how you're appearing
- The thought: "What do they think of me?"
- Energy pulling back from natural expression into self-monitoring
- The impulse to adjust, correct, and improve your presentation
- A tightening in the chest or throat
- The sense of being watched, even if alone
- The voice of the judge arrives instantly, automatically

The moment of choice arrives unannounced:

- Do you notice this contraction happening?
- Can you feel the flow bending inward?

If awareness enters here—even for a breath—the experience continues without identifying with it. You feel yourself being seen, but don't collapse into the image. Action remains transparent.

If reactivity takes over, the self-image solidifies. You become:

- **The One** who must be right
- **The Two** who must be needed
- **The Three** who must impress
- **The Four** who must be authentic
- **The Five** who must not be exposed
- **The Six** who must be prepared
- **The Seven** who must stay light
- **The Eight** who must be strong
- **The Nine** who must not disturb.

The pattern activates in less than a nanosecond.

Try this:

> Next time you're about to speak in a group, notice the instant before you open your mouth.
>
> - What's happening in that pause?
> - Is there a subtle rehearsal?
> - A checking?
> - A gathering of yourself into an image of competence or casualness or authority?
>
> That gathering is the shock point. The question is not whether it happens—it will—but whether awareness can be present for it.

The Felt Sense of the Second Shock Point

You've been working on something, thinking through a problem, trying to figure out the next step. You've been at it for a while. The effort is real. The mental activity is genuine. But something isn't moving.

You feel yourself tightening around the question. The mind becomes more insistent, more repetitive. You review the same thoughts, the same angles, hoping this time they'll yield something new. There's a sense of strain, of pushing against something that won't give.

This is the threshold between Six and Seven. This is where mental effort meets its limit.

What it feels like:

- Circular thinking that goes nowhere
- The sense of needing to figure it out before you can proceed
- A low-grade anxiety about not knowing
- The impulse to gather more information, ask more questions, plan more thoroughly
- Physical restlessness or mental agitation
- The feeling of being stuck while simultaneously spinning

The moment of choice:

- Do you notice that the thinking has become compulsive?
- Can you feel the effort squeezing tighter?

If awareness enters here, the whole system can exhale. The mind stops insisting and becomes receptive. The question remains, but the grip releases. Something finer than thought—intuition, grace, a shift in perspective—can enter.

If reactivity takes over, the mind either intensifies its grip (Six) or escapes into distraction (Seven).

- **The One** redoubles its efforts.
- **The Two** reaches out for reassurance.
- **The Three** shifts to a different project.
- **The Four** sinks into the mood of stuckness.
- **The Five** withdraws further.
- **The Six** questions everything.
- **The Seven** looks for the next thing.
- **The Eight** pushes through.
- **The Nine** numbs out.

Try this:

> Notice when you're caught in a mental loop—replaying a conversation, planning a difficult exchange, trying to solve a problem that won't resolve. Instead of trying harder or distracting yourself, pause. Ask: "What if I can't think my way through this right now?"
>
> Feel what happens in your body when you stop insisting. Does something soften? Does space appear? That softness, that space, is the portal the second shock point opens toward.

Between Reaction and Recognition

The shock points are not places you arrive at and set up camp. They're thresholds you cross constantly—in conversations, in traffic, in the shower, at the keyboard. Every time the flow of life encounters a natural pause, these moments appear.

The work is not to avoid the pause or transcend it, but to meet it consciously. Not once, but again and again. The pattern will activate. The contraction will occur. Awareness doesn't prevent this; it illuminates it.

Over time, something shifts. The interval between pattern and recognition grows shorter. You catch yourself tightening before the image fully forms. You feel the mental grip before it becomes compulsive. The space between stimulus and reaction—what Viktor Frankl called our essential freedom—becomes inhabitable.

This is how personality loosens its hold. Not by being destroyed but by being seen. Not by effort but by attention. The same thresholds that once produced automatic reaction become the doorways through which presence returns.

Questions for Direct Investigation

These are not questions to answer mentally but invitations to observe what's actually happening:

At the first shock point:

- When do I become aware of being observed by others or by myself?
- What happens to my breathing when self-consciousness arises?
- Can I feel the difference between doing and performing?
- What does it feel like when natural expression turns into self-presentation?

At the second shock point:

- When does thinking become compulsive rather than creative?
- What happens in my body when the mind tightens around a problem?
- Can I sense the moment when effort tips into strain?
- What would it feel like to not know, just for this breath?

In both:

- What's here before the pattern activates?
- Can I feel the contraction happening without trying to stop it?
- What remains present even when I'm identified with the reaction?
- Is there something aware of the whole process?

The shock points reveal themselves through direct observation, not through analysis. Watch for them. They're already here, woven into the texture of your day, waiting to be recognized.

When Two Fields Meet

The Enneagram of personality describes nine ways consciousness contracts into pattern. But we don't live in isolation. Every relationship is a meeting of two fields—two patterns of contraction and opening, two different ways of protecting what matters, two distinct rhythms of defense and presence.

Understanding your type illuminates your inner landscape. Understanding how your type interacts with another reveals the architecture of relationship—where connection flows naturally, where friction arises, and why particular dynamics repeat across different relationships.

What follows is not a compatibility guide. There are no "good" or "bad" type combinations. Every pairing contains both the potential for collision and the possibility of mutual awakening. The question is never whether two types can work together, but whether the two people inhabiting those patterns are willing to meet what arises with awareness.

Reading the Field Between

Before we examine specific pairings, it's worth understanding what actually happens when two patterns meet. Every relationship creates a field—an energetic space where two ways of protecting, defending, and seeking connection interact. Sometimes this field feels spacious and alive. Sometimes it feels contracted and exhausting. Learning to sense the difference is the beginning of a conscious relationship.

The field contracts when both people are operating from their patterns simultaneously. This doesn't require conflict or drama. You can be sitting quietly with someone and feel the air thicken. A subtle resistance enters. Words become effortful. The ease that was there moments ago vanishes. What's happened is that your defense has triggered theirs, or theirs has triggered yours, and now you're both protecting against each other without realizing it. The Eight's strength feels like domination to the Two. The Two's care feels like an intrusion to the Eight. Neither person intends harm, but the fields are pushing against each other.

You can feel this in your body before your mind names it. Your breathing becomes shallow. Your shoulders tighten. You start monitoring your words more carefully. There's a sense of walking on eggshells or pushing against something invisible. The other person's presence, which moments ago felt nourishing, now feels like a demand or a threat. This is the signature of mutual contraction—two patterns defending against each other while each believes they're simply responding to the other's behavior.

The field opens when at least one person recognizes the contraction without reacting to it. This doesn't require both people to be conscious simultaneously. One person's awareness creates space that allows the other's awareness to emerge. The Eight notices its armor forming and softens instead of hardening further. The Two catches themself reaching and pauses. The Six feels the anxiety spiraling and exhales instead of questioning. In that moment of recognition, the field shifts. The air opens. Breathing returns. The other person, who was just experienced as threat or burden, becomes human again.

Why do some relationships trigger your pattern more intensely than others?

Because certain type combinations create what might be called resonant interference—the defensive strategy of one person naturally activates the wound of the other.

- The Five's withdrawal pierces the Two's fear of being unwanted.
- The Three's doing makes the Nine's inertia more visible.
- The One's correction hits the Four's sense of defectiveness.

These aren't personal attacks; they're structural dynamics in which one pattern's defense happens to be the very thing that makes the other pattern contract.

This is why the same pattern can feel manageable with one person and unbearable with another. It's not about compatibility or incompatibility in some fixed sense. It's about whether the specific way you defend happens to trigger the specific way they're wounded, and vice versa. When you understand this, you stop making the other person wrong for "making you" react. You begin to see that your reaction reveals where your pattern is still operating unconsciously, and their presence—precisely because it triggers you—is showing you where awareness needs to enter.

The gift of relationship is that it makes the pattern visible in ways solitary practice cannot. Your partner, your child, your colleague—they're not obstacles to your awakening. They're mirrors showing you exactly where you're still asleep. When you stop resenting them for triggering your contraction and start recognizing the contraction, every relationship becomes an invitation to consciousness.

The Basic Patterns of Interaction

When two people encounter each other, their fields interact in predictable ways based on their core patterns:

- **Adjacent types** (connected by a single point on the circle) often share a quality but express it differently. The One and Two both care about rightness—the One through principles, the Two through care. They recognize something familiar in each other, but the different expressions can feel like a distortion. "Why can't you just be direct about what's right?" meets "Why can't you feel what's needed?"
- **Opposite types** (across the circle from each other) often polarize, each representing what the other has rejected or hidden.
  - Eight and Two: strength vs. tenderness.
  - Five and Two: withdrawal vs. connection.

  The Eight may judge the Two's warmth as weakness; the Two may judge the Eight's strength as callousness. Yet each carries what the other needs to become whole.

- **Triangle types** (3-6-9) in relationship often struggle with visibility. They can feel each other's presence as interference with their primary strategy. The Three wants to act; the Nine wants to rest; the Six wants to question. When all three are in a room, no single force can dominate, and each must learn to include the others.
- **Hexad connections** (types connected by inner lines) create relationships where one person's defense triggers the other's contraction. An Eight-Five pairing: when the Eight intensifies, the Five withdraws. When the Five withdraws, the Eight intensifies further. The pattern spirals unless one of them catches it and brings awareness.

But these are broad strokes. The real texture of relationship reveals itself when we look at specific pairings in depth.

Type Eight and Type Two

Strength Meets Care

On the surface, this pairing can feel complementary. The Eight protects; the Two nurtures. The Eight brings intensity; the Two brings warmth. In presence, they can create a powerful field of grounded love—strength that includes tenderness, care that includes boundaries.

But watch what happens under stress:

The Eight feels vulnerable and armors the heart. The Two, sensing the withdrawal, reaches toward the Eight with increased care. "What's wrong? Let me help." The Eight experiences this as an intrusion and pushes harder. "I'm fine. I don't need anything." The Two feels rejected and either escalates the helping (pulling Two's distorted Four: "You never let me in") or collapses into hurt (pulling Two's distorted One: "After all I do...").

The Eight, meanwhile, isn't experiencing rejection of the Two. The Eight is protecting its vulnerability. But the Two takes it personally, and the Eight's impatience with the Two's hurt reinforces the pattern. The Eight pulls its distorted Five—withdrawing into strategy—which makes the Two feel even more abandoned.

This cycle can repeat for years unless one of them recognizes what's actually happening. The gift comes when the Eight learns that vulnerability with the Two isn't weakness—it's connection. And when the Two learns that backing off isn't abandonment—it's respect for the Eight's autonomy.

When both are present, something beautiful emerges: The Eight's strength protects the Two's open heart without controlling it. The Two's warmth softens the Eight's defenses without demanding access. Power and tenderness weave together naturally.

Type Five and Type Seven

Stillness Meets Motion

This pairing often attracts through complementarity. The Five is drawn to the Seven's vitality and engagement with life. The Seven is intrigued by the Five's depth and quiet knowing. Each sees in the other what they've lost touch with.

In presence, they balance beautifully. The Five grounds the Seven's expansiveness. The Seven draws the Five into participation. Together they create spacious engagement—present but not heavy, free but not scattered.

Under stress, the pattern inverts:

The Seven wants to go, do, and experience. "Let's try this new restaurant! Let's invite people over! Let's plan a trip!" The Five feels overwhelmed and retreats. "I need quiet. I need space. Can we just stay home?"

The Seven experiences this as rejection of life itself. The Five's withdrawal makes the Seven more agitated (pulling Seven's distorted One: "What's wrong with wanting to live?"). The Seven's intensity makes the Five contract further (pulling Five's distorted Seven: mental escape into future scenarios of how to get free).

Neither is wrong. The Seven isn't being selfish; it's trying to stay in contact with aliveness. The Five isn't being withholding; it's trying to preserve the internal space needed for clarity. But without awareness, each person's strategy triggers the other's contraction.

The breakthrough comes when the Seven learns that stillness isn't death—it's where depth lives. And when the Five learns that engagement isn't overwhelm—it's where knowing becomes participation. When both are present, the Five can say "I need space" without the Seven hearing rejection. The Seven can say "Let's engage" without the Five feeling invaded.

Type One and Type Nine

Order Meets Peace

This pairing often forms around a hidden contract: the One will maintain standards; the Nine will maintain harmony. It can work beautifully when both are relaxed—the One's clarity guiding the Nine's receptivity, the Nine's acceptance softening the One's rigidity.

But watch the pattern under stress:

The One sees something that needs correcting—a decision unmade, a plan unformed, something wrong that should be addressed. The One brings it up crisply and clearly, with reasons. The Nine hears criticism and withdraws, not outwardly but energetically. "Mm-hmm. Sure. Whatever you think is best."

The One feels the withdrawal as passive resistance and becomes more insistent. "I'm not being critical. I think we should..." The Nine, feeling the intensity increase, merges further into compliance while internally pulling away (pulling Nine's distorted Six: "I can't do anything right").

The One experiences this as the Nine being lazy or uncommitted (pulling One's distorted Four: "I'm the only one who cares"). The Nine experiences the One as controlling and rigid. Neither sees what's actually happening: the One is trying to create rightness; the Nine is trying to preserve peace. Each person's strategy threatens what matters most to the other.

The transformation occurs when the One recognizes that not everything needs fixing—some things need accepting. And when the Nine recognizes that peace, including engagement, is deeper than peace through avoidance. When both are present, the One can offer clarity without demand. The Nine can offer acceptance without disappearing.

Type Four and Type Six

Depth Meets Ground

The Four and Six can create profound intimacy or endless anxiety, sometimes both in the same conversation. The Four seeks authentic connection through emotional depth. The Six seeks reliable connection through tested loyalty. Both hunger for something real beneath surface relationship.

In presence, they offer each other what they need: The Four brings the Six into feeling, beneath the mental noise. The Six brings the Four into groundedness, beneath the emotional intensity. Together they can create relationships of remarkable depth and faithfulness.

Under stress, the pattern becomes painful:

The Four feels something and wants to explore it. The intensity rises. The Six, encountering that intensity, questions: "What does this mean? Are we okay? Where is this going?" The Six's questioning feels like doubt to the Four, who interprets it as lack of depth. "You're not really here with me."

The Four's judgment triggers the Six's anxiety (pulling Six's distorted Three: compulsive reassurance-seeking). The Six's anxiety triggers the Four's sense of deficiency (pulling Four's distorted Two: "I have to make you feel safe to prove I'm lovable"). The cycle spirals.

Neither is wrong. The Four isn't being dramatic; it's trying to create real intimacy through authentic feeling. The Six isn't being anxious; it's trying to establish safety through understanding. But each person's strategy triggers the other's wound.

The breakthrough comes when the Four learns that not all questioning is doubt— sometimes it's the Six's way of coming closer. And when the Six learns that not all intensity is danger—sometimes it's the Four's way of making contact. When both are present, they can meet in remarkable depth without either losing ground.

The Universal Patterns

Across all pairings, specific dynamics repeat:

- **Pursuit and Withdrawal** - One person's way of creating connection feels like a threat to the other. The pursuer intensifies; the withdrawer retreats. The pattern escalates until someone catches it.
- **Mutual Defense** - Both people are defending against their fear, but each experiences the other's defense as an attack. The Eight's armor meets the Five's withdrawal. The One's correction meets the Nine's compliance. Neither sees their contraction, only the other's.
- **Complementary Contraction** - Each person's pattern triggers the precise thing that makes the other contract further. The Two's helping makes the Eight feel controlled. The Eight's independence makes the Two feel unneeded. The very thing each is doing to solve the problem perpetuates it.
- **Recognition as Portal** - The moment one person recognizes the pattern while it's happening—not in analysis later, but in the live moment—the field shifts. One person's awareness creates space for the other's awareness. The mutual contraction becomes mutual recognition.

Relationship as Mirror

Every relationship shows us where we're still contracted. The places where you consistently struggle with someone aren't random. They're pointing to where your pattern meets its edge, where your defense is still operating unconsciously.

The Eight who keeps encountering "needy" people might ask: What am I defending against by keeping everyone at a distance? The Four who keeps meeting "unavailable" people might inquire: What am I defending against by staying in longing?

This doesn't mean you're creating the other person's pattern. It means your pattern attracts, tolerates, or reacts to theirs in predictable ways. The work isn't to find someone without patterns—everyone has them. The work is to become conscious of how your pattern interacts with theirs.

The deepest gift of relationship is that it makes the pattern visible in ways solitary introspection cannot. Your partner, your child, your friend, your colleague—they show you where you're still asleep. Not through their words about you, but through the automatic reactions they trigger in you.

When you stop making them wrong for triggering your contraction and start recognizing the contraction itself, relationship becomes practice. Every friction point becomes a doorway. Every repeated pattern becomes an invitation to wake up.

Two people who are willing to do this work together create something rare: a field of mutual awakening, where each person's consciousness supports the other's recognition, where love includes seeing clearly, and where presence becomes shared ground.

Working With What You've Discovered

You've seen the architecture. You recognize the pattern. You understand the two shock points—the precise thresholds where consciousness contracts into personality or opens into presence. And now the essential question emerges: what do you actually *do* with this?

The answer is both simple and demanding. You don't begin a new practice. You don't add a technique. You don't invent a method. The doing is already happening. Life continually presents the exact moments where your pattern activates. Your task is simply to notice. The Enneagram does not tell you to try harder; it teaches you where to look while you're already living.

This makes the inner work immediate. You don't wait until you feel ready. You don't wait until you understand more. You meet the shock points as they arise— because you are crossing them dozens of times each day. The question is only whether you are present for them.

You start with what is obvious. If you're a One, the contraction shows up as the tightening that precedes judgment. If you're a Four, it is the moment feeling turns into identity. If you're a Five, it is the instant you begin withdrawing from immediacy. If you're an Eight, it is the bodily armoring that tries to prevent vulnerability. Whatever your type, there is a signature shift in sensation, attention, and emotion.

That shift *is* your work.

Seeing the pattern will not stop the pattern. This is crucial. The One will still judge, the Four will still long, the Six will still anticipate danger, the Nine will still drift. What changes is not the pattern but your relationship to it. The pattern that once happened *as* you begins to happen *in* you. It moves through your awareness without defining you. This shift is subtle but absolute. It is the difference between being imprisoned by your pattern and being the space in which the pattern appears.

And all psychological, spiritual, and self-transformational work is ultimately this: learning to stay present at the shock points.

The Only Places Transformation Happens

Every method—therapy, somatic work, meditation, mindfulness, shadow work, trauma work, spiritual practice—ultimately points to two thresholds.

The first shock point, between points 3 and 4, is where the outward flow of experience bends back into the self. Expression meets interruption. If awareness is present, the pause deepens into insight. If awareness is absent, the pause collapses into self-consciousness, self-image, and identification. This is where the personality structure first takes shape. Every distortion grows from this single turn.

The second shock point, between points 6 and 7, is where the mind reaches its limit. It is the moment when the system must open to renewal or tighten into fear. If awareness is present, this threshold becomes the gateway of grace. If awareness is absent, the system contracts, repeats, plans, anticipates, protects, and exhausts itself. It is the birthplace of anxiety, avoidance, and compulsive attempts to control the future.

Every form of real inner transformation is simply remaining awake at these two points. They are the only places where freedom is possible because they are the only places where we lose it.

Trace any struggle back to its source, and you will always arrive at one of these shock points. Stay present at that exact point today, and the pattern begins to unwind.

But there is one force that interrupts presence at the first shock point more powerfully than anything else. One mechanism that diverts the flow back into personality every time. One internal structure that uses your vitality against you to maintain the old identity.

The superego.

And this is why the next chapter is essential.

Why All Work Ultimately Leads to Superego Work

The moment awareness approaches the first shock point—where real experience could deepen inward—the superego intervenes. It is the internal switchman that diverts the rails. Any movement toward authenticity, vulnerability, depth, immediacy, or reality is instantly redirected into self-judgment, self-correction, or self-improvement.

The superego is the mechanism that says:

- You should be better.
- You should have known.
- You should try harder.
- You should not feel this.
- You should be different than you are.

This one message collapses the entire shock point.

It turns presence into performance, sensation into deficiency, converting emotion into identity; it freezes spontaneity into self-consciousness.

And because the superego is built from childhood emotional residue, it carries an intensity that far exceeds the situation. Its force does not come from accuracy; it comes from unresolved emotion. It is the child's fear, shame, and confusion speaking with the authority of the adult mind.

This is why every path—spiritual, psychological, developmental—eventually leads to superego work. Until the superego is recognized as a mechanism rather than a truth, the shock point cannot open. Presence cannot enter. Awareness cannot complete the arc. The personality will always reclaim the steering wheel.

You now understand:

- what the shock points are
- why they matter
- how patterns activate
- where consciousness contracts
- why recognition—not effort—is the practice
- how every form of growth depends on presence at these thresholds

The next steps are unavoidable.

> To work at the first shock point, you must meet the structure that interrupts it.

> To remain present during contraction, you must recognize the voice that hijacks presence.

> To allow experience to unfold without collapse, you must understand the mechanism that collapses it.

That mechanism is the superego.

And because the superego is built from your past, fueled by unresolved emotion, disguised as your own voice, and deeply woven into your sense of self, it requires its own chapter.

The work with shock points is the architecture. Superego work is the plumbing. It is where the leaks occur, where the pressure rises, and where the system diverts itself back into its old identity.

What follows next is the chapter on superego work—how to recognize it, how to disengage from it, how to meet the unresolved emotion that powers it, how to reclaim your vitality from it, and how awareness dissolves the entire mechanism.

This is the real beginning of transformation.

Superego Work and the First Shock Point

Understanding the Enneagram as a living process changes the entire terrain of inner work. What once looked like nine complex personality patterns collapses into something far more elegant. Everything hinges on two shock points—the precise thresholds where consciousness either continues deeper into experience or bends back into personality. Every psychological, emotional, and spiritual pattern originates at these thresholds. The shock points bring laser clarity to the work. No matter what appears on the surface, the real issue is always the same: the moment awareness leaves the immediacy of experience.

The first shock point is the place where doing meets being. It is where the natural flow of experience encounters interruption and turns back on itself. Instead of continuing inward into presence, experience becomes self-conscious. This is the hinge where the real is lost. It is also the doorway where the real can return.

This is where the superego takes over.

The Superego's Place in Development

The superego is not the beginning of personality. Personality begins much earlier—through the infant's first impressions, frustrations, needs, longings, and relational patterns. These pre-verbal structures form the foundation of the type's orientation to life.

The superego comes later.

It begins forming after age two and consolidates by around age six. It is created through internalizing the emotional tone, judgments, fears, and expectations of parents, caregivers, teachers, and culture. External authority becomes internal authority.

So the superego does not create personality. It enforces it, stabilizes it, guards it, and keeps the early adaptations from changing.

The superego is the internal regulator that keeps the personality looping in familiar grooves. It polices deviation from the identity the child constructed. It redirects anything fresh or real back into the old orbit.

This is why superego work is essential. Without recognizing and dismantling the internal enforcer, the deeper personality structures remain intact, untouched, and unchangeable. Presence cannot enter the first shock point because the superego always pulls the lever first.

Understanding the Superego

The superego is not alive. It has no agency, no intelligence, and does not exist in the present moment. It is a mental construct—a prerecorded loop built from the emotional atmosphere of childhood. Drop the stylus into the groove, and the same music plays every time.

What gives it power is that it uses your language, your emotional history, and your sense of identity. It feels personal because it was absorbed at such a young age. But it is not you. It is an artifact.

Strip away every variation, and the superego has one essential message: *You're lower than whale poop, and you need to fix it.* This arrives with a two-part structure:

- **First, the verdict:** You're wrong, lacking, defective, weak, selfish, too much, or not enough.
- **Second, the demand:** Fix it. Improve it. Correct it. Hide it. Work harder. Be better.

This second part—the demand to do something—is the real derailment. Instead of remaining with experience, the psyche flips into self-correction, self-attack, performance, or collapse.

You can locate the superego instantly by listening for its signature phrase: *"You should"* or *"You shouldn't."* Any message that includes these words is a superego message. It is the pivot that pulls you from presence into self-correction.

But the superego often emerges before language—as a tightening in the body:

- A drop in the belly
- A clench in the jaw
- A sinking in the chest
- A freeze in the solar plexus

The body feels the pressure first. The mind supplies the sentence later. This is the first moment the shock point contracts.

Superego Messages Across the Nine Types

The content of the message varies by type, but the distortion remains the same.

> **Type One:** You should have known better.
> **Type Two:** You're selfish and uncaring.
> **Type Three:** You're failing, and people see it.
> **Type Four:** You're too much, not enough, or both.
> **Type Five:** You don't know enough and will be exposed.
> **Type Six:** You're unprepared, and everything will collapse.
> **Type Seven:** You're missing out and doing life wrong.
> **Type Eight:** You're weak and losing control.
> **Type Nine:** You're insignificant and better off disappearing.

Each of these contains a tiny grain of familiarity wrapped in massive exaggeration. The superego always makes a mountain out of a molehill. It inflates human limitation into catastrophe. It transforms vulnerability into deficiency. It turns ordinary emotion into moral failure.

It is completely disconnected from reality.

This is why you cannot satisfy it. It contradicts itself. It shifts expectations. It raises the bar the moment you reach it. No argument will win. No achievement will quiet it. No amount of self-improvement will silence it.

You are damned if you do and damned if you don't because the superego is not speaking to the present. It is speaking from the past.

The Emotional Glue Holding the Superego Together

Unresolved childhood emotions hold the entire superego structure together. The mechanism is fused with the fear, shame, hurt, longing, helplessness, and confusion that the child could not process. These emotions were too overwhelming for the young nervous system, so the psyche built strategies to contain them. The superego became the enforcer of those strategies.

You are not battling the superego. You are meeting unprocessed childhood intensity.

This is why the superego feels so powerful. It runs on your vitality, uses your essential energy against you, and is fueled by emotions the child could not tolerate.

When the superego activates, your nervous system is hijacked by the past. Your adult body is flooded with the child's emotion. The intensity belongs to a different time, but the body reacts as if it is happening now. This includes maturing your nervous system and expanding your comfort zone (homeostasis).

The real work is to bring your adult nervous system to the situation: to feel what the child could not, to stay present with the intensity instead of acting it out, and to allow awareness to metabolize what was once unprocessable.

Awareness Does the Heavy Lifting

The key to superego work is awareness. You do not defeat the superego through effort. You do not fix it. You do not argue with it. You do not appease it.

You disengage by seeing it.

- Awareness dissolves the glue.
- Awareness drains its fuel.
- Awareness collapses the illusion of authority.
- Awareness allows the emotional residue to surface and release.

This often involves conscious suffering—remaining with the discomfort instead of obeying the familiar demand. You feel the contraction without collapsing into it. You sense the pressure without trying to fix it. You stay open while the old message plays itself out without your participation.

You are resisting the demand you've obeyed your entire life. The demand to fix yourself, improve yourself, reshape yourself, and to stop feeling what you feel.

This is not suppression. This is presence. This is adulthood returning to the scene of the original injury.

When your adult presence holds the child's intensity, the emotional glue begins to soften. The superego loses authority. The entire structure starts to unwind.

Awareness metabolizes what the child could not.

The Later Stages

As the superego loses power, something unexpected happens.

It becomes boring.

What once felt urgent and overwhelming becomes stale and predictable. The messages lose their spell, their umph! The emotional hook dissolves. The entire system feels lifeless because it is nothing but the past replaying itself.

Boredom is freedom. You have stopped feeding the mechanism.

Then humor appears.

The superego becomes funny—absurd, melodramatic, and clueless. The certainty with which it pretends to know what's best becomes laughable. It's like a wacky mother-in-law in the back seat giving emphatic directions while reading a roadmap from fifty years ago.

Humor breaks identification. You see the mechanism for what it is: an outdated tape loop with no clue about reality.

Mapping Your Early Messages

To begin working with the superego directly, take a simple sheet of paper and draw a vertical line down the middle. At the top of the left column, write: You should. At the top of the right column, write: You shouldn't.

Then begin listing everything you should and shouldn't do. Remember from childhood. Include spoken messages, unspoken expectations, habitual tones, emotional atmospheres, and implicit family rules.

You should be polite.	You shouldn't upset your father.
You should be the good one.	You shouldn't need anything.
You should keep the peace.	You shouldn't cry.

Then identify the source. Mark each message with 'Mom,' 'Dad,' or another caregiver.

Not to blame. For accuracy. The superego has a lineage.

This alone creates distance. Distance creates clarity. Clarity opens the doorway to awareness.

Once you map the messages, you begin to see the architecture of your superego. You catch the you should as it arises. You recognize the contraction before the words. You start to feel the emotional glue underneath. And you begin to disengage—not through effort, but through seeing.

The Beauty of the Shock Points

The Enneagram as living process is elegant. It shows that the surface details—stories, moods, conflicts, defenses—are not the real issue. The shock point is. Because the shock point is both the place of derailment and the place of return.

You bring awareness to the moment experience bends back into personality. You reclaim your vitality. You stop feeding the mechanism. You allow presence to enter the threshold where it once left.

And the real comes back online.

Super Ego and the Second Shock Point

Returning to Basic Trust

If the first shock point is the interruption of experience—where the superego bends the flow of life back into personality—the second shock point is the restoration of experience. It is the place where the soul returns to its original ground of basic trust. Basic trust is not an attitude, a belief, or a mindset. It is the soul's innate sense that being is fundamentally safe, that reality is inherently workable, and that the unfolding of experience can be allowed without interference.

The first shock point frees us from the internal coercion that pulls us back into self-image. The second shock point opens the way forward. It invites the soul from vigilance into receptive participation, from control into allowing, from anxiety into presence.

Where the first shock point requires recognition, the second involves surrender.

At the second shock point, the central task is openness—acceptance, patience, availability, tolerance, and a willingness to let experience reveal itself. It is the moment where the soul must relinquish its habit of anticipating the next moment, managing the flow of life, and demanding certainty before entering the unknown.

The essential gesture is simple: we let go of the need to know, the need to control, and the demand that the next moment must be predictable before we meet it.

Control is the final contraction of personality. It is the last line of defense between the soul and its freedom. The second shock point is where that contraction begins to release. The grip eases. The breath softens. The psyche stops bracing against what comes next.

What emerges is intimacy. The soul touches life directly. Experience is no longer filtered through anticipation. Presence becomes immediate.

This is not passivity. It is participation, the pure responsiveness of being without the interference of self-management. It is a return to the soul's original relationship with reality—open, unguarded, and curious.

Relinquishing the Habit of Control

To enter the second shock point, the soul must reacquaint itself with the capacity to let true nature have its way. This means we stop trying to secure the future. We stop rehearsing outcomes. We stop shaping ourselves around imagined dangers. We stop insisting that life unfold according to our plans.

Relinquishing control does not mean becoming careless or unfocused. It means recognizing that the deeper currents of being are already in motion, already guiding, and already expressing themselves. Control is the ego's attempt to substitute its tension for the effortless intelligence of reality.

Letting go at the second shock point is not something you do; it is something you stop doing. You stop interfering. You stop tightening. You stop steering. You stop bracing. The moment control relaxes, the natural movement of true nature flows again.

And with that flow comes something the soul has missed for a long time.

The Return of Discovery

As basic trust reawakens, something essential begins to move through the soul—something older than personality, older than fear, and older than the very sense of identity. What returns is vitality in its original meaning.

Vitality comes from the Latin vitalis, "belonging to life," "life-giving," "essential for life," derived from vita, "life," and from an even older Proto-Indo-European root meaning "to live," "to breathe," "to be alive." This ancient root gives rise to vivid, revive, survive, viable.

Vitality is the animating spark, the breath of aliveness, the inner current that moves life forward.

This is precisely what returns at the second shock point.

> Life gains its breath back.
> Being regains its movement.
> Experience regains immediacy.

This process returns life to the life of discovery.

When the psyche is no longer braced against the next moment—no longer gripping, predicting, scanning, or managing—experience becomes fresh again. You begin to sense the world not as a threat to navigate but as a field of revelation. The heaviness dissolves. The rigidity softens. Surprise becomes possible again.

The thrill of living returns.

Vitality, in its deepest sense, begins to flow freely. The inner atmosphere becomes vivid and awake. The senses open. The edges dissolve. The moment feels spacious rather than narrow. The future feels like an invitation rather than a demand.

The Rebirth of Curiosity

With vitality comes another ancient movement: the insatiable curiosity of reality to know itself.

This curiosity is not the mind's restless search for information. It is the curiosity of being itself. It is existence probing its depth and possibilities through your experience. It is the mystery that discovers itself within the living moment. It is the movement of life awakening to its presence.

When basic trust is restored, this curiosity becomes effortless. You do not force yourself to be curious—curiosity reveals itself as the natural movement of the soul. You do not attempt to animate yourself—vitality rises on its own. You do not chase meaning—meaning emerges from the heart of the moment.

The more control relaxes, the more curiosity flows. The more curiosity flows, the more intimacy with reality deepens. The deeper the intimacy, the more alive the soul feels.

You begin to live inside discovery rather than trying to manufacture it.

> Every moment becomes a doorway.
> Every sensation becomes a messenger.
> Every emotion becomes a revelation.
> Every encounter becomes alive with depth.

Life becomes vivid. Experience becomes participatory. Reality becomes intimate.

The second shock point is not an achievement. It is a return to the:

- soul's original orientation

- openness that was present before fear
- vitality that was present before contraction
- curiosity that was present before control
- basic trust in existence—the quiet confidence that being itself is enough.

Two Shock Points as a Single Living Process

The two shock points are not separate events or unrelated insights. They are one continuous movement of reality expressing itself through the human soul. They mark the two thresholds where experience can either contract into personality or open into being. Together, they form a single process: the restoration of the soul's natural orientation toward reality.

> The first shock point is where experience bends.
> The second shock point is where experience returns.
>
> The first shock point reveals where we lose ourselves.
> The second shock point reveals where we find ourselves again.
>
> The first shock point shows the mechanism of limitation.
> The second shock point shows the possibility of freedom.

Seen together, they form a rhythmic movement in the life of the soul—a living cycle that repeats itself at deeper and deeper levels. The soul learns to recognize the bend, to stay present at the hinge, and to lean into the openness that waits on the other side.

Unhooking from the Past

The first shock point is the moment where presence begins to collapse into personality. It is the exact point of derailment—the pivot where experience turns from direct contact with the moment into self-correction, self-image, expectation, fear, or avoidance. The superego is the mechanism that enforces this pivot.

The first shock point requires awareness—pure seeing. Awareness unhooks the grooves of the past, dissolves identification, and reveals that the superego is an artifact, not a guide.

This is the work of disentanglement. Disengaging from the internal coercion. Allowing the unresolved emotional glue to soften. Letting the adult nervous system meet the child's intensity.

The first shock point frees the soul from the weight of the past.

Returning to Basic Trust

Once the soul is no longer pulled backward by internal forces, it encounters the second shock point—the threshold where the future is allowed to unfold without control.

Here, the work is not disengagement but openness; not observing but receiving; not restraint but surrender; not bracing but allowing.

The second shock point is the restoration of basic trust—the soul's original confidence that reality is inherently safe, workable, and revealing. The moment the need for control relaxes, vitality returns. Life becomes vivid again. The curiosity of being awakens. The soul begins to sense life not as something to manage, but as something to discover.

This is the work of receptivity, letting experience arrive, letting true nature move, letting reality reveal itself.

How the Two Shock Points Work as One Process

The two shock points form a single cycle of transformation:

- Recognition → Surrender
- Disentanglement → Openness
- Awareness → Allowing
- Unhooking → Receiving
- Letting go of the past → Entering the present

They are not sequential steps; they are two movements of the same breath.

> The first shock point removes obstruction.
> The second shock point restores participation.
>
> The first shock point dissolves contraction.
> The second shock point opens spaciousness.
>
> The first shock point exposes what is false.
> The second shock point reveals what is real.

Without the first shock point, the second is impossible. Without the second shock point, the first is incomplete. Together, they allow the soul to move freely—no longer bound by the past, no longer trying to control the future.

The Maturation of Discovery into Realization

Discovery is the first fruit of the second shock point. It is the return of vitality, curiosity, freshness, and openness. But discovery is not the end of the process—it is the doorway to realization.

> Discovery is when life becomes alive again.
> Realization is when the nature of life reveals itself.
>
> Discovery is the thrill of encountering what you did not know.
> Realization is the recognition of what you have always been.
>
> Discovery is the soul exploring reality.
> Realization is reality revealing the soul.

As the second shock point deepens, discovery matures. The initial excitement—the vividness, the wonder, the freshness—settles into a quiet intimacy. Curiosity shifts from novelty to depth. The thrill of revelation gives way to the clarity of recognition.

This is how discovery ripens into realization. What begins as:

- "look at this" becomes "oh… this is what it is."
- "experience is alive" becomes "I am inseparable from aliveness."
- "reality is revealing itself" becomes "reality is recognizing itself through me."

Realization is not an event. It is the settling of discovery into truth. It is the shift from exploring life to being life.

The Eternal Dance

At the deepest level, the two shock points reveal a single truth: reality unfolds through the dance of not-knowing and revelation.

> Not-knowing is the openness of the second shock point. Revelation is the clarity that arises at the first shock point when we return to presence.
>
> Not-knowing is the soul's willingness to meet the moment without preconception. Revelation is the moment reality discloses what the moment truly is.
>
> Not-knowing is surrender. Revelation is recognition.

106

Not-knowing makes space for revelation. Revelation leads naturally back into not-knowing.

This is the eternal dance of reality—an infinite movement between openness and clarity, between mystery and illumination, between emptiness and form. It is the way reality expresses itself in every moment of consciousness.

The two shock points are simply the human reflection of this cosmic rhythm.

The hinge points where truth bends through the soul.
The thresholds where being awakens to itself.

When the soul learns to stay present at the first shock point and open at the second, life becomes a continuous unfolding of this dance:

- The release of the past.
- The surrender of control.
- The return of vitality.
- The ignition of curiosity.
- The revelation of truth.
- The dissolution into mystery.
- The emergence of deeper revelation.

And on and on, without end.

This synthesis chapter closes the arc:

- The two shock points are not obstacles.
- They are invitations.
- They are the natural gates of the soul's unfolding.
- They are the living process through which reality meets itself through us.

Walking Through the Shock Points

Every type meets the shock points in its own way, but the mechanism underneath is always the same. Something interrupts the flow—an unexpected moment, a subtle disappointment, a tiny break in continuity—and the body reacts faster than thought. A tightening, a flinch, a bracing. The reaction is not random; it is driven by one of three elemental emotional currents: anger, fear, or shame. These aren't ordinary emotions, but deep, organizing forces that shape the entire architecture of personality.

At the shock point, this emotional fuel either takes over or becomes visible. If it takes over, the pattern perpetuates—automatic, habitual, self-confirming. If it becomes visible, even for a breath, something loosens. The reaction doesn't vanish, but its grip weakens. Awareness enters. The deeper intelligence that once failed to arrive begins to return.

Each example in this chapter shows a type meeting the shock point in real time: the reactive fuel activating, the contraction forming, and the moment where the fuel can be tolerated rather than obeyed. This tolerance—allowing the core emotion without acting it out or shutting it down—is what transforms the shock point from a mechanical loop into a doorway.

We begin with the One, whose entire structure is driven by anger held tightly inside—anger that must be seen, allowed, and tolerated if the pattern is ever to become transparent.

Point One

Meeting the Shock of Imperfection

Anger Held Inside

An Enneagram Type One is preparing dinner. The timing is precise, the counter clean, everything arranged with care. Then their partner walks in, carrying a pan at the wrong angle, splashing a bit of sauce onto the floor. The moment is small. But inside the One, something sharp ignites.

This is the first shock point—doing meets being—and underneath the reaction is anger. Not explosive anger. Not loud. But compressed anger, the internal pressure that drives the entire Type One structure. It rises instantly: a tightening in the stomach, a narrowness in the eyes, a subtle but unmistakable clench.

Inside, the anger says:

- "This shouldn't have happened."
- "This is wrong."
- "This needs to be corrected."

The anger automatically fuels the next moves. The tone shifts. The jaw sets. The corrective impulse surges into speech: "Please don't carry it like that." The words are calm, but the body is rigid. The pattern perpetuates.

This is anger animating the machinery. But then a pause, a flicker, and awareness touches the tightening.

The One recognizes the anger—not as righteousness, not as moral urgency, but as sensation. It is felt directly. It is *tolerated*. And that tolerance interrupts the compulsion to fix the moment. The anger remains, but it loses its authority. It becomes something happening within awareness, not something that *is* the One.

Now the second shock point becomes possible: knowing must give way to trust. The body softens. The breath deepens. The spill on the floor remains a spill, not a threat to order. The need to correct dissolves, not through effort, but because the anger was allowed to be felt without being acted out.

The One kneels and wipes the floor—not to restore righteousness, but simply because the floor is wet. The action is clean, unburdened, free of the inner tightening.

This is the One meeting the shock point with presence:

- Anger is seen rather than obeyed.
- Anger tolerated rather than suppressed.
- Anger allowed to lose its grip.

Here, the pattern stops perpetuating. Here it begins to become transparent.

Point Two

Meeting the Shock of Disconnection

Shame Reaching Outward

A Two is finishing a long day. Their partner walks through the door tired, drawn inward, barely making eye contact. The Two moves toward them immediately—warmth on their face, hands already reaching to help, questions ready to bridge the gap. But the responses come back short and flat.

Then the shock point hits as a tiny break in connection, a flicker of distance, or a subtle pulling away.

Underneath the reaction is shame.

Not the obvious kind, but the deep, existential shame that says:

- "If they turn away, something in me must be unworthy."
- "If the connection falters, I must restore it."

The shame appears as a quick collapse in the chest, a soft sinking inside the heart. Before awareness arrives, shame fuels the reflex: give more. Smile more. Soften more. Become what the moment seems to demand:

- "Are you okay?"
- "Can I do something for you?"
- "Tell me what you need."

The partner's withdrawal increases. Shame deepens. The pattern perpetuates. Then something interrupts, a breath, a slight slowing.

The Two feels the ache under the reaching. For the first time, instead of escaping it, they tolerate it—not fixing, not proving, not earning, and just letting the sensation be there.

In that tolerance, a new quality enters: curiosity.

The Two gets curious about the shame. Not "What's wrong with me?" or "How do I make this go away?" but "What is this… really?"

Curiosity softens the shame's urgency. It creates room—room to sense the texture of the ache, its warmth, its poignancy. The Two notices they have never actually stayed with this feeling long enough to understand it. They always moved past it too fast.

So, they take the next step, they explore it as if for the first time. What is this:

- softness in the chest?
- longing?
- delicate place inside that feels exposed when connection falters?

As they explore, the shame begins to lose its authority. It becomes simply a sensation—alive, tender, almost innocent. The pressure to give collapses, the need to secure love dissolves, and the heart, freed from strategy, settles.

Now the second shock point opens. The Two sees their partner clearly—not as a judge of their worth, not as a source of affirmation, but simply as another human being having a difficult moment.

The Two sits beside them, quiet, present, uncomplicated. There is no performance now, no reaching, no self-forgetting—just presence.

> Shame was the doorway.
> Tolerating it allowed entry.
> Curiosity made space.
> Exploration revealed the innocence underneath.

This is the Two meeting the shock point consciously: not by offering more, but by finally staying with themselves. What arises is the real heart of Two: love that isn't a strategy, but presence offered freely because the One offering it is no longer lost.

Point Three

Meeting the Shock of Inadequacy

Shame Turning into Performance

A Three is delivering a project update. The room seems engaged, the pacing is smooth, the delivery crisp. Everything is calibrated—until someone at the far end of the table says, lightly and without malice, "We may need a bit more clarity in that last section."

> It's nothing.
> But for the Three, it's everything.

This is the first shock point: the instant when doing meets being, when the performance suddenly becomes visible rather than seamless.

And underneath the reflex, shame flashes to life.

Not the outer, social shame of a misstep, but the more profound, identity-level shame that says:

- "If I falter, the whole image falters."
- "If the image falters, I disappear."
- "If they saw something unclear, maybe they saw *me*."

It hits like a small implosion in the sternum—heat rising in the chest, breath constricting, attention narrowing to the task of restoring excellence as fast as possible.

Shame fuels the reflexive script: smooth it over, brighten the tone, reassert competence.

"Absolutely—I can refine that section. Already noted."

The voice is confident, but the breath is tight. The persona is intact, but the person has receded. Shame is driving the machinery.

The pattern perpetuates.

Then—something unexpected. A micro-pause. A fracture in momentum.

The Three feels the tightening behind the smile. And instead of overriding it with more performance, they let it be felt. They tolerate the shame. Not as evidence of failure, or a demand for correction, but as sensation—raw, warm, vulnerable, strangely alive.

Tolerating it interrupts the reflex. The drive to repair the image loses its force.

And in the newly created space, curiosity emerges.

The Three gets curious about the shame:

- "What is this… actually?"
- Not "How do I fix it?"
- Not "How do I look good again?"
- But "What is this small collapse inside trying to show me?"

Curiosity softens the armor. It slows the performance impulse. It turns the moment inward rather than outward.

Then the Three does what the personality has never allowed: they explore the *felt sense* of shame—its warmth, its collapse, its quiet ache—as if touching it for the very first time.

> What is this tender ache?
> What is this sense of exposure?
> What is this quiet longing to be valued without achievement?
> What if there is a self here—beneath all the doing?

As they explore, the sense of shame shifts. It becomes less of a threat and more of a portal.

The second shock point begins to open: knowing must give way to trust.

The Three no longer needs to restore the image. The body softens. The breath returns.

The remark becomes simply a remark—not a verdict, not an X-ray of inadequacy. The persona loosens, and presence comes forward.

Shame was the doorway. Tolerating it interrupted the performance.

Curiosity opened space. Exploration revealed the person beneath the facade of the achiever.

This is the Three meeting the shock point consciously: not by dazzling, not by compensating, not by proving worth, but by allowing the shame and discovering that nothing essential was damaged.

Here, the pattern stops perpetuating. And the radiance that returns is no longer fabricated—it's real.

Point Four

Meeting the Shock of Being Unseen

Shame Turning into Longing

A Four is sharing something personal—nothing dramatic, but genuine: a feeling, an insight, a moment from the day that mattered to them. They speak with care, wanting connection, wanting resonance. Their friend listens kindly but responds with something light, brief, not quite attuned.

And the Four feels it immediately—the shock point. A sudden drop in the heart, a tightening behind the eyes, a familiar sense of being missed.

Underneath the reaction is shame.

Not the shame of failure, but the more profound shame of invisibility:

- "If you didn't understand me, maybe I'm not understandable."
- "If you didn't meet me, maybe I'm not meetable."
- "If you didn't feel me, maybe my depth is too much—or not enough."

This shame rises as a tender ache, an emotional sinking that feels like the beginning of longing. It fuels the reflex: intensify, deepen, reach for emotional impact. The Four expands the feeling, adds nuance, heightens the expression—trying to be found through depth.

The friend grows quieter. The Four grows more expressive. The pattern perpetuates.

Then—something interrupts. A slight pause. A soft awareness.

The Four feels the ache under the drama. And instead of weaving meaning around it, they let the ache be present. They tolerate the shame—not as proof of defectiveness, not as confirmation of being misunderstood, but simply as sensation. The longing loses momentum. The emotional wave softens.

And in the quiet that follows, curiosity appears. The Four gets curious about the shame:

- "What is this tender pull inside?"
- "What is this ache trying to protect?"

- "What if this feeling isn't a flaw, but simply something to be felt?"

Curiosity begins to unwind the narrative. It turns the moment inward rather than outward.

Then the Four moves toward the one thing they've always avoided: they explore the felt sense of shame—its softness, its warmth, its vulnerability—without amplifying it, dramatizing it, or turning it into an identity.

They explore it as if touching a fragile flower they've never allowed themselves to hold.

And as they do, something shifts. The shame becomes transparent. The longing unravels. The rawness reveals a sweetness underneath.

This is the second shock point opening: knowing gives way to trust.

The Four sees their friend again—not as someone failing to meet them, but simply as another person with their own emotional bandwidth in the moment. The need to be understood softens into the capacity to remain present even when the depth is not mirrored back.

Shame was the doorway. Tolerating it softened the story.

Curiosity opened space. Exploration revealed the tenderness beneath the longing.

This is the Four meeting the shock point consciously:

- not by intensifying emotion
- not by seeking resonance
- not by amplifying their depth
- but by allowing the simple ache of shame to be felt—quietly, without turning it into who they are.

In that allowance, the pattern stops perpetuating. And the depth that returns is no longer a performance—it is the natural depth of presence.

Point Five

Meeting the Shock of Intrusion

Fear Pulling Away

A Five is working quietly at their desk. The room is calm, the mind spacious, the task absorbing. Then someone appears at the doorway—a coworker, a partner, a child—wanting to talk, ask a question, or share something. Nothing dramatic. Just presence. Just proximity.

And immediately, the first shock point hits—a tightening in the solar plexus. A mental flinch. A sudden sense of being *entered.*

Underneath the reaction is fear.

Not panic. Not terror. But the deeper, existential fear of being overwhelmed, intruded upon, or consumed—fear that whispers:

- "If I give myself here, I will lose energy I can't get back."
- "If I engage now, I'll be drained."
- "If I let them in, I might disappear into them."

It rises as a quick contraction behind the ribs, a retreating impulse in the chest, a subtle pulling back of attention. A reflex: to withdraw, create space, and protect the boundary. The Five minimizes expression—short responses, small movements, and eyes lowered.

"What's up?" said in a tone just flat enough to signal distance.

The visitor senses the boundary. The Five's mind begins calculating escape routes. The pattern perpetuates.

Then—something interrupts. A pause. A slight moment of noticing.

The Five feels the contraction directly. And instead of detaching further, they tolerate the fear—not as a demand to retreat, not as evidence that they're about to be swallowed, but simply as sensation: a tightness, a flutter, a warm protective wall.

Tolerating it interrupts the withdrawal reflex. Space appears *inside*, not just outside.

Curiosity comes forward—quiet, tentative, but unmistakable.

The Five gets curious about the fear:

- "What is this tightening inside?"
- "What is this instinct to pull away trying to protect?"
- "What happens if I don't immediately retract?"

Curiosity loosens the grip on the boundary. It makes the inner world porous rather than defended.

Then the Five does something the personality rarely allows: they explore the felt sense of fear—the contraction, the guardedness, the subtle tremor of uncertainty.

They explore it as if encountering a shy animal—gentle, cautious, respectful of its sensitivity.

And as they do, something shifts. The fear becomes less threatening. It reveals itself as sensitivity, not danger. The boundary softens from the inside.

This is the second shock point opening: knowing gives way to trust.

The Five doesn't suddenly overshare or merge. They simply remain present *without withdrawing from themselves*. The visitor is seen clearly—not as a threat to autonomy, but as a person with a simple need in the moment.

The Five responds—briefly, authentically, without losing contact with themselves. No drain. No collapse. No disappearance.

Fear was the doorway. Tolerating it interrupted withdrawal.

Curiosity opened the boundary. Exploration revealed the sensitivity beneath the defense.

This is the Five meeting the shock point consciously:

- not by shutting down
- not by disappearing
- not by rationing connection
- but by allowing the fear to be felt—quietly, directly—until it loses its command.

The pattern stops perpetuating, resulting in the natural clarity and spaciousness of the Five—open, present, and still intact.

Point Six

Meeting the Shock of Uncertainty

Fear Spinning into Vigilance

A Six is preparing to leave the house—keys in hand, bag packed, everything seemingly in order. Then a thought flashes across the mind, small but sharp: "Did I lock the back door?"

> It's nothing.
> It's everything.

This is the first shock point: the moment where knowing falters and uncertainty slips in. And underneath the reaction is fear—not loud fear, not apparent fear, but the more profound existential fear that whispers:

- "If I don't check, something bad might happen."
- "If something happens, it will be my fault."
- "If I trust myself and I'm wrong, I won't recover."

The body reacts instantly: a tightening in the gut, a slight surge in the chest, a subtle narrowing of attention; a pattern of scan, question, prepare, doubt, recheck.

"I'll just make sure." The Six walks back toward the door. The pattern perpetuates.

The mind begins its familiar spiral:

- "What if I didn't?"
- "What if I thought I did?"
- "What if someone breaks in?"
- "What if I'm being careless?"

Fear animates the machinery. Then—something unexpected. A pause. A flicker of inner noticing.

The Six feels the contraction. And instead of obeying it, they tolerate the fear—not as demand, not as evidence of danger, but as a direct sensation:

- a tightness in the ribs

- a flutter in the chest
- a vibrational hum of uncertainty.

Tolerating it interrupts the need to recheck. A crack opens in the spiral.

Into that crack, curiosity appears.

The Six gets curious about the fear:

- "What is this tightening inside?"
- "What is this impulse to double-check protecting?"
- "What if I simply feel this uncertainty instead of solving it?"

Curiosity softens the vigilance. The mental spin slows. The breath widens.

Then the Six takes the next step—the one the personality fears most:
they explore the felt sense of fear—the trembling, the shakiness, the instability—
without turning it into a problem to fix.

They explore it like someone holding a bird with trembling wings—gently,
respectfully, allowing the fear to be itself.

And as they do, something shifts.

The fear reveals itself not as danger, but as sensitivity—an attunement to what
could go wrong, rooted in care, not catastrophe. The need to check dissolves. The
capacity to *be with* uncertainty emerges.

This is the second shock point opening: knowing yields to trust.

The Six discovers they can act without perfect certainty. They can move forward
with awareness, not vigilance. They can feel fear without obeying it.

The back door remains unchecked—and the world does not fall apart.

Fear was the doorway. Tolerating it interrupted the spiral.

Curiosity softened the doubt. Exploration revealed the sensitivity beneath the
alarm.

This is the Six meeting the shock point consciously:

- not by bracing
- not by confirming

- not by securing safety
- but by allowing the fear to be felt—fully, intimately—until it releases its grip.

Resulting in the Six's real gift: grounded, intelligent trust that includes fear rather than eliminating it.

Point Seven

Meeting the Shock of Limitation

Fear Escaping Into Possibility

A Seven is making plans for the weekend—ideas flowing, excitement building, possibilities branching effortlessly outward. Then a small obstacle appears: a friend cancels, the weather shifts, or a long-forgotten obligation suddenly matters. It's minor. Ordinary. But for the Seven, it's the first shock point.

> A faint pressure in the chest.
> A tightening behind the smile.
> A quick internal recoil.

Underneath the reaction is fear.

Not fear of danger, but the deeper existential fear of being trapped, stuck, closed in—fear that whispers:

- "If this door closes, I'll lose my freedom."
- "If I'm limited, I'll lose my joy."
- "If I stay here, something bad might happen inside me."

This fear rises as a subtle flicker—barely noticeable unless they pause, triggering reactivity to escape into options, imagination, stimulation, and the future. The Seven's mind leaps ahead instantly:

"Well, we could do this instead! Or that! Or maybe—oh!—I've been wanting to try…"

The excitement ramps up, but underneath it, something is tightening. The pattern perpetuates.

Then—unexpectedly—a slight pause, a slowing of the mental pivot.

The Seven senses the flicker beneath the enthusiasm. And instead of leaping away from it, they do the simplest—and hardest—thing: they tolerate the fear. Not as a threat, or as a cage, but as sensation—a quiver, a fluttering, a warm unease in the belly.

Tolerating it interrupts the flight. The escape does not launch. And curiosity arises.

The Seven gets curious about the fear:

- "What is this restlessness inside?"
- "What is this nudge to move away?"
- "What happens if I don't jump to the next possibility?"

Curiosity softens the momentum. The internal pressure loosens. The mind stops sprinting toward the next thing.

Then the Seven moves closer—something the personality never allowed: they explore the felt sense of fear. They feel the buzzing under the ribs, the emptiness that stirs when options fade, and the subtle panic of stillness.

They explore it gently, as if discovering a part of themselves they've always outrun.

And as they do, something shifts. The fear becomes less frightening. It shows itself not as a trap but as an invitation to presence—a doorway into the richness of the moment they were about to flee.

This is the second shock point opening: knowing gives way to trust.

The Seven sees the changed plan without catastrophe. The limitation becomes spacious rather than confining. The moment becomes enough.

Fear was the doorway. Tolerating it paused the escape.

Curiosity opened space. Exploration revealed the tenderness beneath the restlessness.

This is the Seven meeting the shock point consciously:

- not by distracting
- not by reframing,
- not by spinning possibilities
- but by allowing the fear of limitation to be felt—directly, delicately—until it loses its urgency.

In that moment, the pattern stops perpetuating, and joy arises not from freedom from the moment but from freedom *in* the moment.

Point Eight

Meeting the Shock of Vulnerability

Anger Surging into Control

An Eight is in a conversation—direct, engaged, feeling the natural strength of presence. Everything is straightforward until someone says something unexpectedly personal: "I felt hurt when you said that." The words are simple. Honest. Offered without blame.

But for the Eight, this is the first shock point. A sudden opening in the chest. A flash of exposure. A moment where the ground feels too close, too soft.

Underneath the reaction is anger. Not loud, aggressive anger, but the deeper, primary anger that protects the Eight from the unbearable sensation of vulnerability—anger that whispers:

- "Don't let this soften you."
- "Don't let them close in."
- "Don't be caught off guard."

It rises instantly as heat in the belly, a forward movement in the body, a subtle hardening behind the ribs creating ground to push back, take charge, redirect, overpower the moment.

> "That's not what happened."
> "You're being too sensitive."
> "You misunderstood."

The tone sharpens. The energy intensifies. The pattern perpetuates.

But then—something interrupts. A tiny slip in certainty. A moment of unexpected awareness.

The Eight feels the heat, the tightness, the instinct to dominate. And for the first time in this moment, they tolerate the anger—not feeding it, not acting from it, not suppressing it, but simply feeling it as sensation: a fire in the belly, a protective surge in the chest.

Tolerating it interrupts the reflex to control. A small clearing opens inside.

Into that clearing comes curiosity—quiet, unfamiliar, but unmistakable.

The Eight gets curious about the anger:

- "What is this heat in my chest?"
- "What is this push forward protecting?"
- "What if I don't armor up right now?"

Curiosity softens the fight. It slows the surge. The body stops leaning forward.

Then the Eight does what the personality has never trusted: they explore the felt sense of vulnerability beneath the anger. They feel the shakiness under the strength, the tenderness just beneath the heat, and the small, almost innocent softness that anger has been guarding their whole life.

They explore it as if encountering a part of themselves they were told never to touch.

And as they do, something shifts.

The anger reveals itself not as aggression, but as protection—born from care, not threat. The need to take charge loosens. The Eight stays present without pushing.

This is the second shock point opening: knowing gives way to trust.

The Eight hears the other person again—not as challenger, not as opponent, but as someone expressing real emotion. And the Eight, grounded and unarmored, responds with clarity and presence: "I didn't know you felt that. Tell me more."

No loss of strength. Just the strength that can afford to soften.

Anger was the doorway. Tolerating it halted the push.

Curiosity opened the armor. Exploration revealed the tenderness underneath.

This is the Eight meeting the shock point consciously:

- not by dominating
- not by asserting
- not by controlling the narrative
- but by allowing the anger—and the vulnerability under it—to be felt, fully and directly.

This returns Eight to their true power: strength that includes tenderness, presence that doesn't need protection.

Point Nine

Meeting the Shock of Disruption

Anger Flattening Into Numbness

A Nine is sitting on the couch at the end of the day, finally settling into the soft hum of comfort. The room is quiet, the body unwinding, the atmosphere warm and undemanding. Then someone enters—a partner, a roommate, a child—and says something mildly charged: "We need to talk about that thing from earlier."

Nothing harsh. Nothing dramatic. But for the Nine, this is the first shock point.

A ripple in the stillness. A slight tightening in the chest. A subtle sense of being *pulled out* of themselves.

Underneath the reaction is anger.

Not fierce, not explosive—the Nine rarely feels it that way. But the subtler, instinctive anger that arises whenever the flow of ease is interrupted—anger that whispers:

- "This is too much."
- "Don't disturb the peace."
- "Don't make me come forward."

It appears as a faint pressure behind the sternum, a heaviness in the limbs, a quick impulse to retreat into softness or dissolve into the background. Activating the unconscious pattern to numb out, smooth over, downshift attention, disappear from the moment.

"What's wrong?" said gently, but with the hidden hope that the conversation would fade away.

The body slumps slightly. The mind drifts—the energy drops. The pattern perpetuates.

The Nine withdraws into comfort—into the familiar haze where nothing feels sharp enough to require full presence.

Then—something interrupts. A brief noticing. A small jolt of clarity.

The Nine feels the inner collapse. And instead of sinking into it automatically, they tolerate the anger—not expressed outwardly, not denied, but felt directly as a pressure in the chest, a slight heat under the softness, a subtle tightening that wants to go numb.

Tolerating it interrupts the dissociation—the haze thins. A faint outline of presence emerges.

Into that space, curiosity flickers. The Nine gets curious about the anger:

- "What is this weight in my chest?"
- "What is this impulse to fade?"
- "What am I afraid of meeting right now?"

Curiosity lifts the fog. The internal contraction becomes clearer. The impulse to withdraw slows.

Then the Nine does what the personality rarely allows: they explore the felt sense of anger as if discovering it for the first time. They feel the heaviness, the warmth, the quiet pressure that never found a voice, and the boundary beneath the placidity. They touch the fire that has always lived under the water.

Exploring it reveals something startling: Anger is not dangerous—

- It is aliveness.
- It is vitality.
- It is the energy of engagement the Nine has been avoiding.

And as they explore, something shifts. The collapse stops. The numbness recedes. The body wakes up.

This is the second shock point opening: knowing gives way to trust.

The Nine turns toward the one who spoke—not with avoidance, not with passivity, but with steady presence. They maintain their ground, their voice, their connection to themselves.

"I'm here. What's going on?" No collapse. No drift. No disappearing.

Anger was the doorway. Tolerating it prevented withdrawal.

Curiosity opened the fog. Exploration revealed the strength beneath the softness.

This is the Nine meeting the shock point consciously:

- not by fading
- not by accommodating
- not by dissolving
- but by allowing the quiet anger to be felt—gently, directly, until it becomes vitality.

The true gift of Nine: presence that is calm, grounded, and fully alive returns.

If you want to explore these same shock points as they first appear in childhood—before they became the adult patterns you now inhabit—*The Enneagram World of the Child* offers a deeper lens. It traces how the primary emotions of anger, fear, and shame shape early personality, how the superego seizes them to form the inner voice you now take for granted, and how curiosity—the most natural quality of the child—remains the key to loosening the whole knot. Understanding how these forces arise in the beginning gives adults a profoundly compassionate perspective on their patterns. It reveals how the same innocence that first contracted can become the doorway to freedom.

Applying the Process

Other Paths of Transformation

The Diamond Approach® as a Working Example

When the Enneagram is understood as a living process rather than a personality map, something essential becomes clear. The same inner mechanics operate in every authentic path of transformation. Whether you work through the Enneagram, the Diamond Approach®, somatic inquiry, contemplative traditions, or depth psychology, the underlying structure of awakening remains constant—the language changes. The practices change. The metaphors change. But consciousness moves through the same universal rhythm of reactivity, contraction, space, essence, and embodiment.

The Diamond Approach as a Working Example

The Diamond Approach is a helpful example not because it uses the Enneagram structurally, but because its experiential method reveals the same geometry the Enneagram describes. You see the same turning points, the same descent into the structure of self, the same openings into spaciousness, and the same movement of essence coming forward to reorganize experience.

This is especially apparent in psychological process and therapeutic work, where the living process becomes unmistakable. Beneath every modality lies the same architecture of human transformation. Every method has a point where the flow of experience tightens into reactivity. Every process has a moment when attention is guided toward the underlying structure of that reaction, and an opening when something fresh, real, and unconstructed begins to reveal itself.

The Enneagram makes this architecture visible. It shows that what therapists call projection or activation, what somatic practitioners call contraction or bracing, what contemplative traditions call ego-clinging, and what the Diamond Approach calls object relations are all movements within the same lawful rhythm.

The First Shock Point

In the Diamond Approach, inner work begins exactly where Gurdjieff's Enneagram of Process locates the first shock point: the moment of reactivity.

Something happens. A comment lands. A familiar tone of voice hits a nerve. A feeling flares up. This is where most people collapse into their habitual pattern.

In the Enneagram's geometry, this is the interval between Points 3 and 4, where outward movement encounters interruption and energy begins to turn inward. This is the birthplace of identification. In the Diamond Approach, this same moment is met with an invitation to simply stay with your immediate experience. Presence entering here prevents the collapse into personality and reveals the deeper structure beneath the reaction. The contraction becomes a doorway. This is the first conscious shock.

The Descent Through Conditioning

Once presence touches the reactivity, the deeper structure begins to open. You begin to sense how the current situation activates something old, something that formed long before you had the capacity for reflection. This descent mirrors the Enneagram's inner hexad, where energy moves from Point 1 to 4 to 2 to 8 to 5 to 7. The psyche reveals itself according to a hidden lawfulness when met with presence. The content is personal, but the structure is universal.

Emptiness and the Second Shock Point

If you stay with the unfolding of this inner structure long enough, something loosens. The grip of identification weakens, and awareness expands around and within the contraction. In the Enneagram, this corresponds to the movement from Point 5 toward Point 6, where the mind unwinds into not-knowing. This space is the opening to the second shock point.

When you remain inside this emptiness without moving away from it, an essential quality arises. It arises spontaneously when the contraction releases and awareness is present. The Enneagram locates this moment in the interval between Points 6 and 7, where a finer energy enters the system, and the process renews itself. The Diamond Approach calls this the arising of essence.

Embodiment and Return

As essence permeates your being, the process naturally shifts into expression. This aligns with the Enneagram's movement from Point 7 to 8 to 9 and back to 1. The presence grounds in the body, saturates awareness, and becomes the seed of new action. Your responses become less reactive and more spontaneous. The Diamond Approach calls this embodiment. The Enneagram of Process calls it the completion of the circle. Both describe the same phenomenon: presence returning to the life of the individual.

The Universality of the Living Process

The Enneagram, understood at its deeper level, is not a typology but an architecture of transformation. The two shock points, the descent into conditioning, the arising of space, the emergence of essence, and the embodiment of presence, are universal movements of consciousness. The form of suffering may differ. The content of personality may differ. But the structure of liberation is the same. It follows an inner law, the same universal laws of manifestation through which anything emerges, unfolds, dissolves, and reappears at a higher octave.

A Final Encouragement for Practitioners of Any Path

If you are a therapist, counselor, coach, or working within another path or modality, consider exploring your approach through the lens of the Enneagram as a living process. Every method has its own two shock points. Every therapeutic system has moments when experience collapses into a pattern and moments when a finer energy enters.

Understanding these universal structures can help you see where a client's process shifts, where the flow contracts, and where awareness wants to enter. Seeing your method through this lens can deepen your precision, clarify your timing, and increase the effectiveness of your work. It allows you to understand not only what is happening in a session, but why it is happening, and how consciousness is trying to move forward.

Reflection

The shock points reveal something essential: the soul is continuously morphing, always opening, always returning. What we call personality is only the moment where that movement paused. What we call awakening is simply the movement beginning again.

The first shock point shows where we turn away from ourselves. The second shows where we return. Together they restore the natural rhythm of the soul.

When awareness meets the tightening of the first shock point, the past loses its claim. When openness meets hesitation, the future loses its hold. What remains is the living present—clear, intimate, and alive with possibility.

Here, the soul rediscovers vitality in its original sense: life breathing through life. Here curiosity awakens—not as a trait, but as the movement of reality probing its depth. Here, discovery ripens into realization as the boundary between inner and outer dissolves.

The Enneagram, in this light, is not a map of types but a diagram of living process— the movement between contraction and openness, between forgetting and remembering, between not-knowing and revelation. It mirrors the way reality moves through us, the way being reveals itself through every moment of experience.

> Nothing needs to be achieved.
> Nothing needs to be perfected.
> Nothing needs to be resolved.

When the soul recognizes its rhythm, the circle completes itself. The pause becomes transparent. The movement begins again. And what once appeared as personality becomes simply one expression of a far greater unfolding.

> Awareness is the returning.
> Openness is the unfolding.

And the dance between them is how reality remembers itself through you.

Final Thought

When this process is seen at its most minute scale, something essential becomes clear: it is unfolding continuously, moment by moment. Every time attention drifts, every moment we slip into memory or anticipation, the same sequence continues—but now within the confines of the constructed self. It moves far too quickly for the mind to track consciously.

Working with the Enneagram as a living process, then, isn't about catching every microscopic shift. It's about recognizing the larger arcs—the movements big enough to sense, feel, and stay with. When presence meets these broader patterns, the flow begins to change. Over time, presence develops its own gravity.

There comes a point when presence no longer needs to be remembered or summoned. It begins to draw us naturally. The process does not stop; it simply becomes transparent. The machinery of the self continues turning, but we are no longer inside it. We are here.

The Inner Architecture Trilogy

The three books in this trilogy form a single unfolding journey: from the machinery of personality, to the transformation of perception, to the living process that reveals who you truly are beneath the patterns. Each book stands alone, but together they create a seamless arc—how the self is formed, how it is seen, and how it is liberated.

Why Study Personality? opens the door. It reveals the architecture of identity, the three centers, and the hidden workings of the mechanisms that shape your inner world before you ever knew you had one.

The Alchemy of Perception deepens the descent. It shows how seeing is not passive but creative—how every moment is shaped by the way awareness meets experience. It refines the instrument of perception so the world can be encountered directly, without distortion.

The Enneagram as Living Process completes the arc. It presents the Enneagram not as a typology but as a living map of consciousness—how Being moves, forgets itself, and remembers. It shows how personality arises as an interruption in a much larger rhythm, and how the same rhythm contains the way home.

Together, these books offer a unified approach to awakening:

- a psychology with a soul
- a spirituality grounded in experience
- a map that brings all three centers—mind, heart, and body—back into a single field of knowing.

This trilogy is for anyone who senses that personal growth is not about becoming a better version of the pattern, but about rediscovering the one who has never been defined by it.

Understanding a child's inner world.

EnneagramWorldOfTheChild.com

About the Author

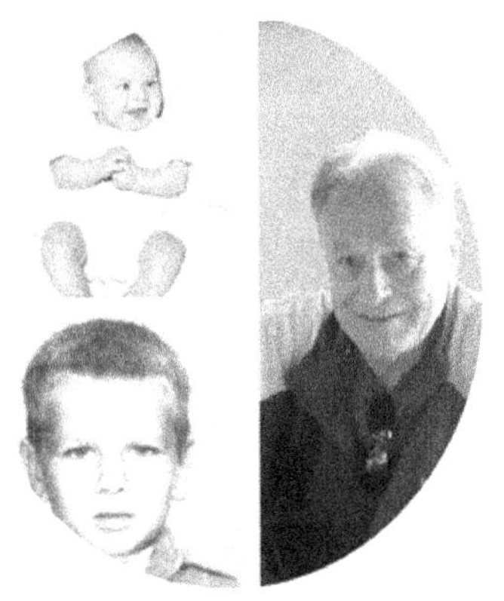

John Harper is a Diamond Approach® teacher, Enneagram guide, and student of human development whose work bridges psychology, spirituality, and deep experiential inquiry. His published books include *Nurturing Essence: A Compass for Essential Parenting,* which invites parents to discover the role essence plays in child development.

He is also the author of *The Enneagram World of the Child: Nurturing Resilience and Self-Compassion in Early Life* and *Good Vibrations: Primordial Sounds of Existence,* available on Amazon.